Sunset
Camping
Handbook

By the Editors of Sunset Books and Sunset Magazine

Special Consultant: John Robinson

Lane Books · Menlo Park, California

Contents

Edited by Cornelia Fogle

Fifth Printing May 1973

*All rights reserved throughout the world.
Third Edition. Copyright © 1970, 1962, 1957
by Lane Magazine & Book Company,
Menlo Park, California.
Library of Congress No.: 72-100895.
SBN Title No.: 376-06203-7.
Lithographed in U.S.A.*

*COVER: New Brighton Beach State Park, California.
Photograph by William Carter.*

ILLUSTRATIONS by Dinah James.

Special Features

PHOTOGRAPHERS

William Aplin: pages 12, 95. **George Ballis:** page 38. **Clyde Childress:** pages 32 (right), 65. **Glenn M. Christiansen:** pages 4, 7 (left), 81, 87. **Clifford A. Fenner:** page 73. **R. A. Fisher:** page 6 (left). **Mike Hayden:** page 6 (right). **Martin Litton:** pages 9, 13. **Ells Marugg:** page 92. **Ken Niles, Jr.:** page 89 (top). **Tom Riley:** pages 32 (left), 80, 82. **John Robinson:** pages 8, 34, 71, 84, 89 (bottom), 93. **Bob and Ira Spring:** page 11. **W. D. Stammers:** page 77. **Blair Stapp:** page 70. **Darrow M. Watt:** pages 7 (right), 40, 69. **Elton Welke:** page 68. **Robert Wenkam:** page 19.

Introduction

The simple living and carefree atmosphere of camping appeals to more people each year as today's busy world grows more complex. Daily cares rapidly drop away as you listen to rushing water cascade noisily down a rocky creekbed, watch a squirrel scamper unafraid through your campsite, smell the morning coffee and frying bacon which signal the start of another day.

Campers come in all ages, shapes and sizes. The entire family can find it a refreshing change and, thanks to modern innovations, camping can be as comfortable and convenient as you wish.

What kind of camper are you? Do you prefer to try different sites or to relax in one spot? Do you like to rough it away from other people or to enjoy an accessible site in an organized camp ground? Do you want sleeping and cooking arrangements to be as comfortable as possible, or do you feel that you aren't really camping if you don't cook over an open fire?

Camping has had a tremendous growth in the past few decades, and to capitalize on the camping boom, industry has been working overtime on new ideas to make camping easier and more luxurious.

But if camping becomes *too* easy and luxurious, many of the good things it gives us can be lost— the feeling of self-reliance gained from coping with primitive conditions, the stimulation of the outdoor environment, the child's appreciation of unfamiliar wildlife, the testing and stretching of muscles in rugged country. Good camping skills preserve all these values, yet make camping fun.

IT'S NAPTIME for these preschool campers, as they stretch out on air mattresses with favorite toys. For lightweight blankets, use beach towels.

Camping equipment . . . a booming business

The tremendous explosion in the camping equipment field has popularized camping as never before. The wide range of equipment offers the individual many options from which to select those suiting his particular interest. The camper who grew up in the traditionalist school may reject many of these devices—but where once only the hardy camped, now all kinds of people are camping. Their common urge is to enjoy themselves, and they have many ways of approaching it.

Only a generation or two ago, camping was of an entirely different nature. Whole families— grandparents, parents, children—would set up camp together near some scenic beach or lake not too many miles from home, and spend a week or two on a vacation for the entire clan.

For others, camping was an expensive pastime, with primary emphasis on hunting or fishing camps. Groups of men traveled together by train to a wayside stop where they were met by a guide and his helpers. Food and equipment were provided, and the party traveled either by horse or canoe to a spot pre-selected by the guide. There the sportsmen could pursue their sport unfettered by such mundane problems as setting up tents, building fires, or cooking.

Today these campers have been succeeded by millions, and camping has become regimented— usually restricted to specified areas because of fire danger and the problems that would result from uncontrolled site selection. Forest fires started by uncontained campfires have taught us the value of prepared fireplaces (now found in most public campgrounds) and have also encouraged the development of the portable campstove.

Automobiles bring the wilderness nearer

More than any other single factor, the automobile has had the greatest influence on camping in

HUNGRY CAMPERS concentrate on food rather than the view in this camp in California's Trinity Alps.

FISHERMEN are ardent campers. Many of the best lakes and streams are far from organized camping areas.

America; it brought the far-off wild places within easy reach. The natural result was an ever-increasing demand for suitable roads to get to them. Then, as access to the camping regions was provided, the vehicles began to cut up the trails and raise dust. We now have campgrounds laced with asphalt roads and marked parking spaces, almost like subdivisions. Such campgrounds make the traditionalists sneer, but people with vehicles like them because the ready accessibility makes it possible to carry virtually unlimited equipment directly to the campsite.

In very recent years we have seen what might be called the second generation in camping equipment—the pickup campers, the many kinds of auto trailers, and the motor home. (They have grown out of the first generation kind of auto camping in which the camper loaded his equipment into his car, drove to the campsite, unloaded it and set it up.) These specialized vehicles bring to the campsite what is in effect an already-set-up camp, providing not just shelter and a sleeping place, but in most cases many other refinements.

The evolution of this almost infinite range of camping equipment has brought with it an equally varied approach to camping. People who would not have given camping a second thought a generation ago now happily camp on their vacations and on weekends, because they can do it nearly as luxuriously as they live at home. With today's wide choice of equipment, you may define "camping" quite differently than your neighbor.

Why camp?

You may camp for a change of scene, to enjoy a period of relaxation—in sight of high mountain peaks, beside a blue lake, above a secluded beach, alone in the desert—in an environment completely different from your usual one. The fresh air you breathe and the spacious feeling of sun and sky may be the only rewards you seek.

Teaching children to enjoy the out-of-doors is a motivation for many families. Once it was reasonably cheap to send them to summer camps, but these have become increasingly expensive. Family camping is a shared experience that knits the group. It helps your children gain assurance in a strange environment. It can teach them the rudiments of conservation and an understanding of wild life. It develops them physically at the same time they are learning to enjoy activities such as swimming, hiking, and fishing.

For some groups, the camp is a secondary consideration, functioning mainly as a base where

HIBACHI provides variation from regular camp stove or fireplace meals.

CHILDREN SHOULD HELP with chores. One sweeps camper's "patio," as another goes fishing. Tent provides extra children's bedroom.

they can eat and sleep. Daylight hours are absorbed in pursuit of activity—boating or waterskiing for some, hiking or mountain climbing for others.

Fishermen form another group of inveterate campers. They roam widely—almost always on their vacations, often on weekends—searching out the best places to fish. Many of them find the pickup campers most satisfactory for their mobility and labor-saving conveniences.

We still have millions of acres of unspoiled land in the country, and millions more in Canada, but great sections of it are inaccessible. Additional campgrounds are being built each year, but camping's increasing popularity keeps the demand about equal to the supply. Some campgrounds are deluxe, going so far as to provide hot water showers and flush toilets, but most are more primitive. Competition for the deluxe and most accessible sites sometimes gets fierce; but on any given day, even at the height of the season, thousands of sites are vacant throughout the United States.

Developing good camping skills

Learning to be a good camper is like learning to be a good cook or a good gardener. You learn how to get the best use out of a campsite, how to

be comfortable in camp, how to eat well without undue effort—and how you can do all these things without having to load up on non-essential equipment. As your skills increase, you will open up new horizons in enjoyment of the outdoors.

When you know how to organize for your trip ahead of time, preparation is greatly simplified. The secret is to know what to take along, and how to use it when you get there.

In this book we explore the many possible ways you can camp today. We make plain the advantages and disadvantages of the various kinds of equipment to help you in selecting those items you feel you will need, either for luxury camping or roughing it. We describe in considerable detail the various camping vehicles offered, and provide information on how to match engine power to weight, how to maintain the vehicle, how to load it, how to drive safely.

But our main concern is not with the kind of equipment or vehicle you choose. This is a handbook on camping, not on vehicles; its primary purpose is to help you to enjoy your camping experience after you get to the site. We approach camping as an outdoor sport, in the belief that developing good camping skills is a challenge which successfully met brings satisfaction far beyond the effort required.

Kinds of camping

There are places where you can reserve a camping trailer for a certain date, then on that date arrive at your selected campground, pick out your campsite, and telephone for delivery of your trailer. The rental agency staff will transport it to your site and spot it exactly where you want it. At the end of the rental period they will come and take it away.

The trailer probably will be fitted with a complete set of utensils, LP gas tanks filled for the stove, and everything clean and ready for use. All you will have to bring are your personal effects, clothing, and food.

YOUNG BACKPACKERS set out on a trip into high country. Heaviest part of load is on top, rests on shoulders.

At the opposite end of the scale, and in the same vicinity, you may see several people drive up in a small car and pull into a parking space. They remove their prepared packs, lock the car and within five minutes disappear up a mountain trail. On their backs they carry everything they will need for a two week's sojourn in the high country, completely out of touch with civilization.

Today's camper has a wide variety of choices between these two extremes. Ordering a camping trailer delivered to your selected site costs more than some of us care to spend. On the other hand, backpacking into the high country is not everyone's cup of tea.

CAMPING WITH YOUR CAR

For most of us, at least the first few times, camping is linked to the family car—either a conventional passenger model or a station wagon.

It is not necessary to think in terms of special vehicles for camping. (See later section on recreational vehicles.) If your family is large you may have a station wagon already because of its extra seating capacity, but camping is perfectly practical with the average family sedan. Trunks are roomy, and when carefully packed will swallow a much larger load than you think possible. There is usually considerable extra space on the rear ledge and under the feet of the back seat passengers. (Sleeping bags go well here, for instance.) If you still need more room, you can rent a roof rack or small utility trailer at moderate cost.

Condition of the roads you plan to travel should be considered before you load your car. If your selected area is accessible over well-paved roads and highways, you can obviously carry more weight than you should attempt if you are going into remote places.

It is wise to take it easy until you get the changed feel of your car with the additional weight. The car will tend to sway more and not steer so freely.

Driving in remote areas

In less accessible areas, particularly in the mountains, you may have trouble with heavy loads unless your car is large and powerful. Traffic use on mountain roads does not justify costly modernization, so they are usually winding with steep grades. Road maintenance may be poor, too.

Mountain roads are slow. Plan on triple the traveling time you would ordinarily allow to cover the same distance on a high-speed highway. Curves must be negotiated at reduced speed with a loaded vehicle, and grades will also slow you down. You may get trapped behind trucks and cars towing house trailers.

On a narrow roadway you must stay strictly on your side, since sight distance is usually short. The mountain driver who is lulled into carelessness by lack of traffic may find himself in a frightening and dangerous position if suddenly confronted by a loaded logging truck coming down grade.

Many mountain roads edge along steep slopes, sometimes with awesome dropoffs on one side. This is the only way mountain roads can be built without prohibitive expenditures. They may be disturbing if you are not accustomed to them, but they do not have to be dangerous. The drivers who come to grief on such roads are apt to be the natives who drive them so often they become careless, or those trying to make up lost time.

Roads in remote areas often are not well marked. You will usually discover an error soon enough, but it may be difficult to turn around. In unfamiliar country you can expect to make an occasional wrong turn.

Anyone who has tried to use a two-dimensional map in three-dimensional country knows how difficult it sometimes is to relate the map to the country. This is another reason to allow adequate time. The driver who finds himself on a strange road, still miles from his chosen camping area with night coming on and a carload of irritated passengers, may wish he had never left home.

Less traveled roads may be unpredictable. A broad, well-engineered highway may suddenly deteriorate to a narrow, steep, winding route simply because a planned modernization program is funded over many years.

Camping away from the crowd

Camping in the high mountains or other remote regions has some drawbacks, but it also has its pleasures. If you prefer to get away from the crowd, the difficult access sharply curtails the number of people venturing away from well-traveled roads.

The feeling of tremendous open space is stimulating, and you will find yourself taking deep breaths of the clean air. Although young people adapt to high altitude more quickly than older ones, almost everyone benefits from a sojourn in thinner air. Light exercise such as a short hike in the rarefied atmosphere is as valuable as a gymnasium workout, and much more pleasant.

Wide open spaces also hold their dangers and should be approached with respect. The unspoiled country still preserved is little changed from the days when only the Indians roamed it. Adults sometimes get lost in these primitive areas, while children often do—especially the younger ones who have not developed a sense of direction and are unaware of the dangers of straying from camp.

Temperature fluctuates tremendously in the high mountains, particularly in late spring and

MOST PUBLIC CAMPGROUNDS include fireplace, table with benches. This hike-in camp has these facilities.

fall. The thin air heats and cools rapidly, and a warm 75° day can become a freezing 32° night. If you don't have a camping vehicle, you will certainly want good sleeping bags and a tent, and possibly one of the efficient little heaters now available. Those who enjoy winter camping in the desert experience the same temperature extremes.

Large campgrounds

For gregarious families the large campgrounds are popular. They may range from sea level, possibly on the ocean or close by it, up to altitudes of seven or eight thousand feet in the mountains. Sites in a single campground may number a hundred or more. A highly scenic area often boasts several campgrounds.

Such places take on a resort atmosphere. Children gather in groups to play or splash in the nearby lake or river. Families with neighboring campsites may get acquainted and socialize.

Access is easy, and vehicles come and go. Well marked trails in the vicinity afford scenic hiking, and a concessionaire may be nearby to provide horses and a guide for organized trail rides. Even rental bicycles may be available. Catchable fish are probably stocked in the surrounding lakes and streams, so that there is considerable fishing activity. To the young the capture of a ten-inch trout is an exciting accomplishment. Power boats may be allowed, but more often water craft are restricted to rowboats, sailboats, and canoes because of the noise and danger to swimmers.

Although good roads make it easy to bring in heavy loads of supplies, the preparation of your supply list is not as vital to the success of the trip as in the wilder spots. With so many campers coming in, there is almost certain to be a market within a few miles, or even an old-style general store with a small stock of everything from groceries to fishing lures.

You might ask: Why not depend entirely on the nearby store? Some campers do, bringing only basic staples. But the selection is often limited, and due to the short season and long supply lines, prices will be considerably higher than you are accustomed to paying.

These popular campgrounds usually have better facilities than the remote camps. Rest rooms often have flush toilets. Plenty of water faucets are set at convenient locations, and in some camps even showers are provided. There may be marked na-

ture trails and natural history museums. Most national parks and some large state parks have excellent natural history exhibits, with park naturalists, movies, and naturalist-guided hikes.

The disadvantages of such campgrounds are the obvious ones—they are busy and noisy in the daytime, although at night they quiet down quickly. In the summer season they are usually full, making sites difficult to find. Most of them offer a wide choice of activity, however, and they provide a good training ground for the new camper.

Small cluster camps

Another very common type of campground is the small cluster type found widely in the national forests. Often secluded in groves of trees adjacent to a stream or small lake, they have fewer facilities but more privacy. The cluster may consist of only a few developed sites, with probably a chemical toilet, a single water hydrant, and the usual tables and fireplaces for each site.

A half-dozen or more clusters may be provided at different elevations along a mountain stream. Scenery and natural features may not be as spectacular as at the larger campgrounds, but these small camps afford pleasant surroundings in a more primitive atmosphere. They may offer boating and swimming, and almost always fishing and hiking. Car-camper families favor them, but many recreation vehicles will be found there, too.

Although their total visitor use is not so impressive as in the larger campgrounds, there are many more of them. They are found virtually everywhere in our national forests at all altitudes, and campsites are usually easier to obtain. They are perfectly suitable for the inexperienced camper, though they may require some careful planning on food and equipment.

A special kind of camping has grown up around large lakes and many reservoirs in the West. Although not so intended in the beginning, many of these areas have become boaters' camps. Unless you are a boater or a water-ski enthusiast, they are not particularly desirable for camping because of the noise and ceaseless activity.

Camping on the move

Another special type is travel-camping. In this kind of camping you take whatever site you can find near the end of the day of driving and stay two or three days, exploring the country. Rising early on the day of departure you drive to a new site. This method is uniquely adapted to scenic areas such as the Golden Circle country of southern Utah-northern Arizona where there are many magnificent national monuments and parks deserving more than a quick drive through. The major disadvantage is the great amount of packing and unpacking, which requires keeping your outfit to a minimum. Travel-camping is one reason the recreation vehicles have become so popular.

Sometimes these travel-through campers will stop at a motel for a hot shower and a restaurant meal. Reservations are desirable, but not really necessary unless you want one particular place. Except in the most popular vacation spots at the height of the season, you can usually get a room if you stop fairly early in the day. Out of season, reservations are seldom needed.

CARRYING YOUR CAMP ON YOUR BACK

The most strenuous kind of camping involves backpacking, which opens vast, unspoiled areas to the hiker that few flatlanders see. You must carry everything you will need for the length of time you will be gone. Recommended load for the average male in good physical condition is up to 40 pounds, for a woman or husky pre-teenager up to 30 pounds, and for younger children according to their ability. Strong, experienced backpackers may carry more, but the point is each family must prune its equipment and food to a weight and size that can be carried in backpacks.

Backpacking is merely mountaineering, which has been popular in Europe much longer than in the United States. Weight-saving has become almost a fetish in this sport, and a fascinating range of lightweight equipment is available from stores specializing in backpacking supplies. Few of the items used by the average auto camper are adaptable to backpacking, although much equipment used for backpacking can be used for regular camping.

This does not mean you should buy mountaineering equipment for ordinary camping. It is less convenient to use, and some things are more expensive. Mountaineering stoves are tiny one-burner affairs; tents, if carried, are small and cramped or may be just a plastic tarp. Lightweight sleeping bags are quite costly, since they must be

PACK ANIMALS to carry equipment is deluxe way to see the high country. You can rent riding horses or hike.

made of high quality goose down. Good boots are a must.

LET AN ANIMAL CARRY THE LOAD

Or, as a compromise between auto camping and backpacking, you can hire the services of a professional packer; they are available all over the West. Costs will vary, depending on what you want, but even for deluxe service they should be less than you would pay at an average resort. Included would be a riding horse and pack animal for each member of the party, a guide or packer, and a cook, if desired. Twenty miles a day is the maximum in rough country, but this is much farther than you can go on foot.

You can shave these costs considerably if you are willing to walk. Packers don't like to let their riding stock go out on a trip without one of their own men along, but a pack mule which can carry 150 pounds can be rented for about $7 a day if the trip is several days' duration. Burros are cheaper, but they carry less.

With a little experimenting, you and your family will find the kind of camping that suits you best.

Where are the best campgrounds?

At least once a year, camping families face two big questions: Where shall we camp this year, and what shall we take this time?

Some campers have a simple answer to both questions—they visit the same spot each summer, and they take along an unchanging assortment of gear and food.

But many families get almost as much enjoyment from figuring out where to go and what to take as they do from the camping trip itself. Long before time to leave, they delight in planning new adventures for themselves and finding new country to explore.

DESERT CAMPING is gaining in popularity. Go from late fall to early spring, carry your own water and fuel.

To find an ideal vacation spot, begin your planning early. Study maps, brochures, and camping directories; write to rangers and park superintendents; talk shop with other camping enthusiasts; and follow camp notes in regional magazines and newspapers. Preliminary study doubles the fun of your trip.

Time limits. In the more remote campgrounds you may be able to camp as long as you wish, but in the popular ones campers may find a restricted time limit during the vacation season.

(For a comprehensive list of public campgrounds in the West, see Sunset's *Western Campsite Directory*. Time limits, if any, are included.)

CAMPING SEASONS

Summer is the camping season throughout the United States, but it varies by geographic location and elevation. Campgrounds near sea level and in mild-weather areas open earlier and remain open later. In some places you can camp from April to October, and even November. Camping is at its best during the fall and early winter months in the desert regions of the Southwest.

Campgrounds at high elevations or in brisk climates open late—in June or early July—and frequently close early in September because of snow or cold.

In Mexico you can camp all year. Best weather is between November and April, with the rainy season from May to October. A tourist card is required, except for visits less than 72 hours. You can bring camping gear, fishing equipment, or boats without a special permit, but you will need a permit for firearms. Mexico has few developed campsites.

Canada, like the United States, offers camping primarily in the summer. You need no passport but must carry proof of identification. Sports equipment, including camping gear, boats, and

WHENEVER POSSIBLE, public campgrounds are located near water. This one is along the Merced River in Yosemite National Park. The best campsites fill up rapidly.

cameras, is admitted without special papers, but must be declared upon entry and reported out when leaving the country. A visitor bringing in firearms or fishing tackle does not need a permit, but he must provide Canadian customs with a description of the equipment and serial numbers of the guns. Revolvers, pistols, and full automatic firearms are prohibited. Hunting and fishing are governed by provincial laws, and licenses are required.

WHERE TO GO

You have a wide choice of public and private campgrounds from which to choose.

National parks and monuments

Campgrounds in the national parks and monuments are located in the midst of some of the most spectacular scenery in the country.

For information about a particular national park or monument, write to the park superintendent.

Camps are well equipped with water, tables, and fireplaces; rest rooms are adequate; and there are often such extra facilities as showers and a laundromat. Since the national parks are set aside to preserve outstanding historical, geological, or scenic attractions, there is much for the camper to see and do during his stay. Each park features museums, exhibits, and naturalist services to explain the phenomena to the public. Usually there are restaurants, stores, post office, shops, and resort accommodations.

Campgrounds within the parks are extremely popular, particularly on weekends and holidays.

National forests

Most campgrounds in the national forests are found in mountainous regions, usually between 3,500 and 10,000 feet elevation. On the Pacific coast, a few forests grow down to sea level. Administration is under the Forest Service (U.S. Department of Agriculture).

In campgrounds the Forest Service provides tables and benches, fireplaces, water supply, and sanitary facilities. Additional conveniences may be offered in some of the largest camps. In many of the forests there are lodges where meals and supplies may be obtained.

Many improved campgrounds are now "Charge Recreation Sites", where a moderate fee is charged for camping or picnicking.

National forest camps have many advantages for the camper. Some of the best fishing, hunting, boating, and hiking country is located within their boundaries. Most of the campgrounds are along rushing streams and rivers, or on the shores of mountain lakes. Others are situated on the outskirts of national parks and monuments.

Camping in unimproved areas. Only a fraction of national forest acreage has been developed. Can you camp outside these improved areas? The answer is yes and no.

In general, the Forest Service disapproves of camping outside established areas because of fire hazard and sanitation; in certain regions—such as Southern California—it is expressly prohibited.

If you wish to camp outside improved areas, write to the district ranger in that section of the national forest and ask about the possibilities. Or you may inquire of the ranger or his fire guard when you arrive in the forest. However, don't be surprised if your request is refused, particularly during forest fire season.

Wilderness and primitive areas

Under the Department of Agriculture, the Forest Service is entrusted with the administration of about 100 wilderness, wild, and primitive areas. Most of these are in untouched high-mountain country, and most are in Western national forests.

A new category, wild and scenic rivers, is now being developed.

Total acreage in wilderness and primitive areas is nearly 15 million. No roads may be built in them, no motor vehicles are allowed, nor is commercial timber cutting permitted. You may fish (within state laws), camp, and hike in these areas as you please, but only hikers, horses, and pack animals are permitted. Campfire permits are required. There is an extensive network of trails, but no facilities.

National recreation areas

These areas (including national seashores and lakeshores) are spacious land and water areas that have both recreation qualities of national significance and high-quality natural environments. In general, they are distinguished from national parks by their recreation orientation; most of them border water areas where swimming, water skiing, fishing, and boating are available.

Most of these areas have resulted from water storage behind large dams. Administration is generally under the Forest Service or the National Park Service.

All of the areas have camping facilities, some of high quality. In warmer areas most are boat-oriented. Fees may be expected.

FOREST SERVICE REGIONAL OFFICES

For information about camping in the national forests, write to the Forest Service regional offices at the following addresses:

ALASKA REGION (*Alaska*)
Federal Office Building, P.O. Box 1628, Juneau, Alaska 99801.

PACIFIC NORTHWEST REGION (*Oregon, Washington*)
P.O. Box 3623, Portland, Oregon 97208.

CALIFORNIA REGION (*California*)
630 Sansome Street, San Francisco, Calif. 94111.

SOUTHWESTERN REGION (*Arizona, New Mexico*)
517 Gold Ave. S.W., Albuquerque, New Mexico 87101.

NORTHERN REGION (*N.W. Idaho, Montana, N.W. Washington*)
Federal Building, Missoula, Montana 59801.

INTERMOUNTAIN REGION (*Idaho, Nevada, W. Wyoming, Utah*)
Forest Office Bldg., 324-25th St., Ogden, Utah 84401.

ROCKY MOUNTAIN REGION (*E. Wyoming, Nebraska, South Dakota, Colorado*)
Federal Center, Bldg. 85, Denver, Colorado 80225.

EASTERN REGION (*Illinois, Indiana, Michigan, Minnesota, Missouri, New Hampshire, Ohio, Pennsylvania, Vermont, West Virginia, Wisconsin*)
710 N. 6th Street, Milwaukee, Wisconsin 53203.

SOUTHERN REGION (*Alabama, Arkansas, Florida, Georgia, Louisiana, Kentucky, Mississippi, North Carolina, South Carolina, Tennessee, Texas, Virginia*)
50 Seventh Street N.E., Atlanta, Georgia 30323.

Public lands

Public domain lands are those federally-owned lands which are not dedicated to any specific use by Congress. About 450 million acres of public domain land remain in the United States, mostly in the West and Alaska.

A large portion of these public domain lands are desert, but there are also hundreds of sizable, unsuspected enclaves in superb scenic country. Armed only with a campfire permit, you can use these lands for camping, hiking, rock-hunting, or any other non-destructive activity you care to pursue.

Rules are simple. The required campfire permit can be obtained without charge from many federal agencies. Observe good campfire precautions. Get permission to cross private property. Leave gates as you find them—open or closed. Don't harass livestock. Observe state hunting and fishing laws. Don't litter.

Since many of the public domain enclaves are off the beaten track, they may be hard to find and have difficult access. The Bureau of Land Management has offices in most Western cities.

Information on federal areas

Each major federal agency has many branch and division offices throughout the country. You may find an office listed (under U.S. Government) in your local telephone book if you live in a sizable town or city; or you may direct inquiries to the agency headquarters in Washington, D.C. The Forest Service is part of the Department of Agriculture; under the Department of the Interior are the National Parks Service, the Bureau of Land Management, the Bureau of Reclamation, and—as a coordinating agency—the Department of Outdoor Recreation.

Begin to collect your information early—the agencies won't be so busy, and you may find new avenues of information to pursue.

State park camps

Most state park camps are found at lower elevations, many of them at sea level. They are usually near major roads. Many are located near water—a stream, river, lake, or the ocean—and others are near some natural feature—a waterfall, cave, geo-logical formation, or grove of redwoods.

Overnight camping is permitted in many of the parks. Generally a fee is charged for each night you occupy a site.

For more information, write to the state park department at the state capital, and tell them you are interested in camping in the state. You can now make advance campground reservations for state parks in California.

Many camps are fully improved. In addition to the usual fireplace, faucet, table, and benches, you may find clean rest rooms, hot showers, and laundry facilities. In some you will also find coin-operated stoves, snack bar, grocery store, or gift shop. Firewood is often sold for a small sum. A ranger-naturalist program is conducted in many of the larger parks.

County camps

An increasing number of campgrounds are being operated by county recreation departments. Many are available only for use by residents of the county, but many others may be used by visitors.

Privately owned forest and reservoir areas

Thousands of excellent campsites are being made available today by utility companies and big lumber companies. In extending the courtesy use of these tracts—often well-equipped campgrounds—they ask only that the users observe good outdoor manners and use caution with fire as they would elsewhere.

Wherever big lumber operations exist, areas may be set aside for public recreation. Many utility companies develop power reservoirs in the mountains and allocate public use areas. Some of these may be heavy boating areas, but most are smaller lakes with forested shores and often good fishing.

Commercially operated campgrounds

Comprehensive guides listing these campgrounds are available at recreational vehicle sales agencies and sporting goods stores. These campgrounds are particularly oriented toward vehicle campers; virtually all will be listed. For more information, write to Kampgrounds of America, Inc., P.O. Box 1138, Billings, Montana 59103. Private campgrounds are also listed in Sunset's *Western Campsite Directory*.

Advance planning and preparation

As departure time for your camping trip approaches, you can make some advance preparations to assemble permits, licenses, and maps you will need; insure your vacation equipment, if necessary; and have the car checked to be sure it is ready for vacation driving.

PERMITS AND LICENSES

You can obtain these in advance if you plan to camp in undeveloped areas, or to fish or hunt.

Fire permit

You will seldom need a fire permit if you plan to camp in an organized campground. You will be expected to use the fireplace provided and/or a camp stove, and you will not be permitted to build a fire elsewhere. Many of the larger areas have group campfire sites where campers gather in the evening for nature talks by park rangers, songfests, or entertainment.

You may be permitted to camp in remote areas of large parks, on undeveloped federal land, in the desert, and in primitive or wild areas; but in all except designated areas you must have a fire permit and carry an ax and shovel.

Permits are available at all national forest headquarters and substations, and at most national park and Bureau of Land Management offices. In some states you can also get them at state forestry and park stations, and at sporting goods and camping supply stores.

Fishing and hunting licenses

Licenses can be picked up ahead of time; they are usually available at sporting goods stores, as well as from forest rangers and game wardens.

If you plan to camp in a different state than your own, write to the state fish and game commission for a copy of the state's current regulations. Out-of-state licenses usually cost more than for residents and will probably be valid for only 10 days or two weeks.

Usually licenses are required for all adults in the party (over 16 years of age). Younger boys who hunt may need a certificate showing they have hunter safety training.

State laws apply on most federal lands.

INSURANCE

You should check over your insurance coverage before a trip, both for your vacation equipment and your vehicle.

Insuring your equipment

All of your camping equipment can be protected either with a floater insurance policy or as part of a homeowner's policy.

The floater policy covers specific items, which must be listed; expensive camera or sports equipment is often covered under this type of policy. If the insured item is damaged, stolen, or lost while in camp or on the trail, its repair or replacement is covered by the policy.

Your homeowner's policy probably has a provision covering you up to a maximum amount for loss or damage to personal effects while traveling. You should discuss your policy with your insurance agent, as you may be protected under some circumstances but not others. You may find your possessions covered while you are traveling, but not in camp. You will probably have to furnish proof of loss and of breaking and entering.

Camping equipment is seldom stolen; most losses are of cameras, sports equipment, and other valuable, easily transported items. Areas frequented by day visitors have the highest theft rate.

Car insurance

If you plan to camp for an extended time in either Canada or Mexico, you would be wise to talk with your insurance agent about your car policy.

All car insurance policies written in this country are applicable in Canada; however some United States insurance firms are not recognized by Canadian provincial governments. Before you drive to Canada, ask your broker to provide you with a "pink card" showing that your car is insured with a company that is recognized by provincial authorities. If your car is involved in an accident, the card will secure your immediate release; without it, you may be detained.

If you plan to camp in Mexico, you should buy a Mexican insurance policy covering liability and property damage for the duration of your stay. You can obtain such a policy from insurance offices located near the border. Short-term coverage is not expensive, and is worth many times the cost if you are involved in an automobile accident.

Trailer insurance

Under most policies, liability and property damage features of your car policy are applicable to trailers. However, fire, theft, and collision protection must be purchased separately.

If you rent a trailer for your vacation, read the insurance provisions—if any—carefully when you sign the contract. Some agencies include insurance protection in the rental fee (at additional charge), but others make no such provision. Your comprehensive insurance does not extend to trailers, so if you wish this protection, you should arrange for a special, short-term policy.

PUBLICATIONS

Up-to-date maps and a few nature guides will be well used during your camping trip.

Maps

For most car campers, oil company maps and the national forest maps available from rangers will be adequate. Auto club members can obtain maps from the nearest club office; some clubs furnish highly detailed maps of recreation areas. State promotion departments will send recreation maps and other literature; some have roadside information stations near the state boundary. Sporting goods stores sell a wide variety of maps for sportsmen and hikers.

If you are curious about the lay of the land where you expect to camp, or if you plan to explore it by trail, you may want to buy some of the detailed topographic maps published by the U.S. Geological Survey. They can be obtained in some camping and sporting goods stores or by mail from the Survey headquarters, Denver Federal Center, Denver, Colorado 80215.

Outdoor handbooks

You and your children will be surprised how much you can learn and how many questions can be answered if you take several nature guides along on your trip. Topics include identification of trees, shrubs, and wildflowers; rocks and geology; regional fish and wildlife; and a guide to the stars.

GETTING THE CAR READY

If you will be camping many miles from a garage or driving over rough roads, you should have the car put through a routine safety check. You should make certain you have all necessary equipment in the car trunk.

Car safety check

You or a professional mechanic should check over the car, paying special attention to tires, brakes, lights, cooling system, steering, ignition, carburetor, fuel system, and battery.

Cold weather camping. If you are camping early or late in the season or at high altitude, you may want to protect the car against the possibility of a cold snap. Make sure the radiator is filled with an anti-freeze solution; the windshield washer reservoir should have a non-freezing solution added. Have the battery checked, and pack tire chains where you can get at them easily.

Emergency equipment

Some campers carry a box of emergency equipment in the car; this is a personal choice. You should carry at least one strong, compactly-rolled tow rope, an emergency can of gasoline, and several emergency road flares.

Assembling your equipment

If you are a newcomer to camping you may be awed by the formidable variety of camping equipment available. Catalogs and sporting goods stores offer an amazing array of choices. Everything looks useful and attractive—and you can silently calculate dollars adding up with alarming speed.

Camping by its very popularity has attracted a large number of manufacturers who want to cash in on a growing market. Many of the items offered have legitimate value, but others are not necessary.

Camping is fun. It should be relaxing and easy. You should take along what you need to be comfortable, to keep dry, to stay warm, to enjoy the out-of-doors, to sleep well, and to eat well. Camping is no fun if you are uncomfortable.

To some extent what you take depends upon where you go; but unless you are far off the beaten track, your campsite probably will have a fireplace with grill, a sizable table with benches, a place to park your car, and space for your tent.

You may want to rent your equipment for the first season. Fees are reasonable, and you can get a complete outfit. You can try out some equipment, observe and talk to other campers, and decide what you want before you make a sizable investment.

Certain items, however, are basic to any camping outfit. When you wish to begin accumulating your own equipment, here are some things to keep in mind.

TENTS

For about $3.50 you can buy a tent which can be erected in a minute or two, weighs only 2 pounds, will sleep two people and keep them dry. It is simply a long plastic tube. You run a rope through it for a ridge pole and tie the two rope ends to trees. Weight of the sleepers inside holds the tent down, so no pegs are needed.

This kind of tent is carried by backpackers who want a lightweight shelter they can transport easily, but which will also allow them to sleep dry if they are caught in a storm.

For the family camper, of course, this tent is completely unsuitable. He wants not only a shelter to keep off any rain, but one high enough to stand erect in. He wants more floor space so he can spread out sleeping equipment and still have room to move around. His tent will give privacy for dressing or changing into swim suits. And it should resist sun, moisture, and wind.

To get a tent tall enough to stand up and move around in, you need a sturdy framework. To provide enough floor space the manufacturer must use a great deal more material. For ventilation he must provide openings with screening, fitted so they can be closed from the inside in bad weather. Depending on size, materials, and design, your camping tent will weigh somewhere between 30 and 60 pounds (with frame), instead of the back-

---

BASIC EQUIPMENT

Below are the basic items you need for a camping trip. Many of them can be rented at moderate cost. Check local sporting goods stores.

- Tent or tarpaulin
- Sleeping bags
- Air mattresses
- Ground cloths
- Cooking pots, pans, utensils
- Dining equipment and cutlery
- Dishwashing equipment
- Flashlights and lantern
- Camp tools
- First aid kit
- Personal equipment
- Camp stove (optional)
- Ice chest (optional)

CAMPERS IN THE 1970's have a wide choice in equipment. Here you see a travel trailer in the background, two types of tents in use, a 4-wheel drive vehicle available for exploring back country.

packer's two. An adequate family tent costs between $60 and $200, depending on size and added options.

A generation or so ago, when all tent design was based on interior support, there were only a few classic types; all tents were variations of these types. The invention of the outside framework gave tent designers much more latitude; today there are literally hundreds of kinds available.

Tent framing

When you buy a tent you undoubtedly will look first at those with the outside framing. They have become so popular, and offer so much variety, that they have virtually driven most of the older kinds off the market.

The principle of outside-frame tents is simple. The framework is erected outside the tent, and the tent is hung from it. Tubular aluminum and fiberglass made this method feasible.

Self-sustaining frames. Some of the exterior frame tents and the pop-ups have self-sustaining frames. In these, the framework—either by spring-loaded members or members in tension in use—forms a rigid structure which needs no staking. These are simple to pitch, and they can be moved around

like a big box once they are set up. These tents are good for camping on rocky or frozen ground. But if a heavy wind comes up, they may go rolling across the countryside like a tumbleweed.

Pop-up tents

These tents have a framework which follows the interior contour of the structure, functioning like the ribs of an umbrella. The framework is spring-loaded, which helps in raising the structure and exerts a constant pressure on the skin to keep it taut. The greatest advantage of pop-up tents is ease of handling; their prime disadvantage is the curved design.

The igloo style has a circular floor which makes it difficult to arrange rectangular-shaped cots and sleeping bags. The quonset type has more floor space, but both versions, unless extra-large, are deficient in head room because of the curving roof. Some have windows and sewn-in floors.

A pop-up igloo tent might be considered as an auxiliary children's sleeping tent.

Tent materials

You will find three fabrics predominating—all of cotton. Army duck, in 8, 10, or 12-ounce weights,

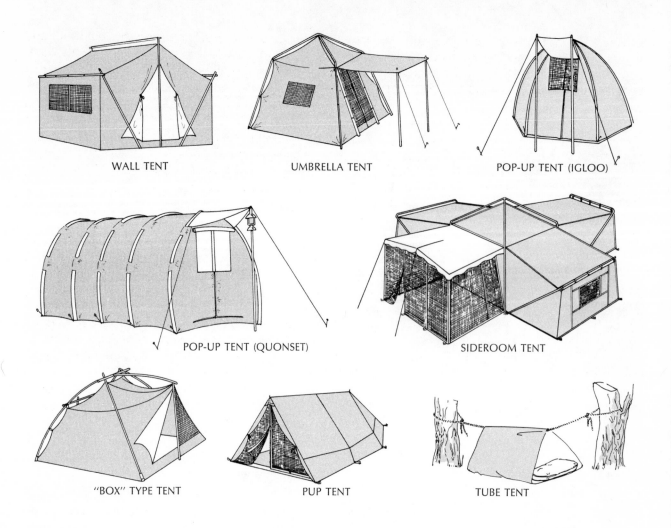

WALL TENT   UMBRELLA TENT   POP-UP TENT (IGLOO)

POP-UP TENT (QUONSET)   SIDEROOM TENT

"BOX" TYPE TENT   PUP TENT   TUBE TENT

is the most durable, but it is somewhat heavier than the other two—poplin and drill—and more expensive. The 8 or 10 ounce weight is best for average use. A variety called shelter duck is lighter and less expensive.

Poplin and drill are most often seen in family tents. The drill should be at least 7.68 ounce weight, and the poplin 6 or 7 ounces. These are lighter materials, less serviceable than duck, but adequate for most camping uses.

Look at tent fabrics carefully. Are they lightly woven, with a hard, twisted thread? Take the material between your fingers. Does it feel as though it would wear, or has an inferior weave been disguised under sizing?

Plastic is used for the backpacker's lightweight tent. It is not very durable in constant use, and over an extended period it deteriorates in sunlight. With both ends open it has excellent ventilation; however, if the ends are closed for warmth and protection, it becomes a sealed space with the same drawbacks as the waterproof sleeping bag.

Waterproofing

All good tent materials can be treated to repel water. Today most tents are water repellent, dry treated, when you purchase them.

In a rainstorm, this treated fabric still permits some air to pass through, but the outside moisture soaks the material, making the fibers swell. At the same time the fabric shrinks somewhat. Both make the material more watertight, but its water-shedding properties depend to a great extent on surface tension.

Don't touch the tent fabric when rain is falling outside—this will start seepage. If too much water collects in some places on the roof, wrap a thick, dry garment around your hand and gently lift the bulging spot.

A completely waterproof tent is impractical. Waterproofing makes the material stiff, and folding to pack and store breaks down waterproofing.

When you get a new tent, set it up in your back yard and wet it thoroughly with the garden hose, leaving the tent up until it is thoroughly dry. This tightens the fabric. Setting up a new tent before you take it camping also helps to familiarize you with the procedure. You will also find out if any essential parts are missing.

Construction

You will probably want a tent with a sewed-in floor; the best ones have nylon floors, vinyl treated. These are easy to keep clean, resistant to rot and mildew.

All fabric junctions should be close-stitched with a double row of stitches, double-lapped.

Stitched grommets are stronger than pressure-attached ones. Make sure the beckets (loops) for pegs and suspensions are attached well; if not securely anchored to a seam they can either pull off or rip the tent.

A raised sill at the entrance to the tent keeps out beetles, mice and chipmunks. This edge of floor makes the tent hard to sweep out. Some tents have zippered sections which can be opened outward for easy cleaning.

Ventilation of your tent is another important point to consider. Too hot an interior is more often a problem than too cold.

Today's tents have much larger windows also. Inside coverings for the windows should be easy to close quickly. Built-in screens for windows and door should be nylon or fiberglass.

Look for the new, indestructible plastic tent stakes in bright colors.

Size

Allow about 27 to 30 square feet of floor space for each person who will use the tent; each cot or sleeping bag will require about 20 square feet. An 8 by 8 foot tent is about right for two people, while four people find a 10 by 12 foot tent about the right size. For more than four people, two smaller tents are more handy than one large one.

You might get one or two small pup tents for children. They don't mind the close confinement, and they are usually delighted to sleep off by themselves.

Tent care

Never pack a tent away wet; be sure it is *completely* dry. If you return from a rainy camping

trip, as soon as possible set up the tent to air and dry out. If it mildews, sponge lightly with water and a gentle-action soap. Scrubbing destroys the fabric's water repellent quality. You can renew this treatment by setting up the tent and painting the water repellent on with a brush, or spraying on from a pressurized can.

Hang the tent if possible, or fold and pack away where it will be dry and away from rodents.

When you buy

As in purchasing any camping equipment, your best guide to quality is to buy a tent made by a reputable company. Your sleeping equipment, tent, and cooking tools are the three most important items. If these are right, your camping experience should be enjoyable, but poor equipment may turn you against camping completely.

Do not approach the purchase of a tent lightly; it will probably be the most expensive single item you acquire. If you carefully select a serviceable, well-made design that you like, with reasonable care it should last many years.

TARPAULINS

Some campers, particularly those who wish to travel light, get along without a tent. Instead they may buy a rectangular canvas sheet with grommets around the edges. Tarpaulins are versatile—they may be used as a tent when strung over a

---

HOW TO PUT UP A TENT

Raising the outside-frame tent is simple. You pick out a level spot and decide where you want the door. Then you rake or sweep the area clear of twigs and rubbish, and remove large surface rocks that could puncture your tent floor.

Spread the floor tautly and stake it down, ignoring the remainder of the structure. When all stakes are in place, you build the framework, slipping the cross members through loops and raising the tent with the frame. With small tents this is a simple process; larger ones may require several steps. However, even the most complicated shapes are easier to raise than the older tents with interior support.

rope, a windbreak when strung between two trees, or as shade over your campsite. You can buy them in plastic, canvas, and other materials—some in bright colors. They are not very expensive and do not take much room when folded.

Many tent owners take along a tarp to use as a canopy over the table or tent entrance, as a windscreen or privacy screen, as litter protection from needles and leaves from overhead boughs, or to shade a play area for small children. Usually you can suspend them from trees on the site, but if you take along some collapsible, lightweight tent poles you can put them exactly where you wish.

Many kinds of canopies, tent extensions, and sunshades are available commercially, but they are usually more expensive than simple tarps; they can be a nuisance in a strong wind.

SLEEPING BAGS

Experienced campers look upon the selection of a sleeping bag as the most critical decision in the process of assembling camping gear. A warm and comfortable sleeping bag can make the difference between an enjoyable camping trip and one best remembered for cold and restless nights.

Before you buy, try to decide what kind of camping you will be doing. You want a bag that will keep you warm and snug through the lowest night temperatures in the country where you plan to camp. High altitude camps need more heavily insulated bags than camps at sea level. If you plan to backpack, you will want to consider light and compact models—making sure they will provide the warmth you require.

There are few bargains in sleeping bags. Quality of materials, design, and workmanship are reflected both in the efficiency of the bag and in how well it stands up to hard use.

Shapes and sizes

Sleeping bags come in two basic design styles: mummy and rectangular.

Mummy bags. The mummy type bag is the favorite of backpackers, and is also a good choice for cold weather campers. The tapered mummy bag fits snugly around its occupant, retaining body heat with minimum insulation.

Many people find them restricting and difficult to get used to. You don't turn inside a mummy bag; it shifts and rolls with you.

Mummy bags are lighter in weight and more compact than rectangular bags because less covering and insulation are required. They are usually more expensive.

Rectangular bags. Most adults prefer the conventional rectangular-shaped bags, which are more comfortable to sleep in. Bags come in a variety of widths and lengths.

The better rectangular bags have a zipper down one side and across the bottom. You can zip two

PITCHING A TARPAULIN

The tarp may be pitched as a tent in a variety of ways. Below are four simple versions based on a piece of canvas 15 by 7½ feet. Sew tent tabs or harness rings on the canvas in the places indicated on the drawings.

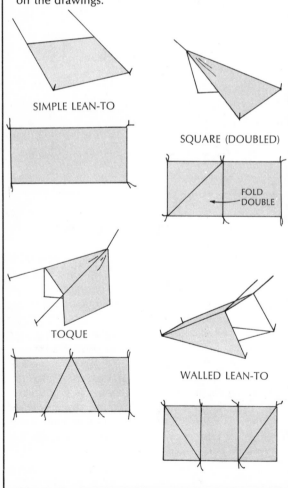

SIMPLE LEAN-TO

SQUARE (DOUBLED)

FOLD DOUBLE

TOQUE

WALLED LEAN-TO

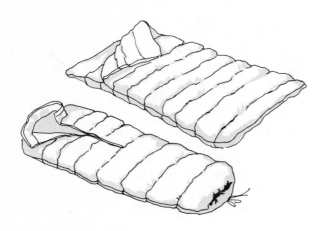

bags together to make a warm and roomy double bag. Good bags have two zipper pulls, one inside and one outside the bag.

Exterior coverings

The cover of a sleeping bag should be a sturdy, flexible material, not easily torn, and one which will allow the bag to breathe—to admit some air and allow moisture to escape. The exterior gets harder wear than any other part of the bag. It is usually tightly woven cotton, or maybe a cotton and synthetic combination. Dark colors—brown and moss green—are easiest to keep clean. Water-repellent fabrics are most desirable for sleeping bag covers. The fibers are treated so they will not absorb moisture from the air and from your body, and openings in the weave are not sealed, so moisture can escape.

A waterproof bag, however, is unsatisfactory. Moisture can't get in, but neither can it get out. Nightly perspiration must pass through the lining, insulation, and covering into the outer air.

Insulation

The effectiveness of the insulation in a sleeping bag is determined by the amount of air that can be trapped within its minute pockets. The desirable characteristics are maximum warmth, light weight, and general durability.

Down fills. The very best, and by far the most expensive, sleeping bags are filled with goose down. Despite recent advances in synthetics, down is still a better insulator than man-made materials.

The most desirable down comes from mature birds raised in cold climates. The feathers are springier and thicker. The finest insulation is 100 per cent new goose down; it gives best wear and most warmth for the weight, and it can be washed and cleaned without any loss in quality. First quality down bags cost from $60 up.

A mixture of goose down and feathers is not quite as efficient as pure down, but is somewhat less expensive. So-called reprocessed down bags may be offered at cut-rate prices, but these should be viewed with suspicion.

Down bags are vital for mountain-climbing expeditions, arctic explorers, and others who go into extremes of cold. The lighter down bags are favorites with high country backpackers, particularly the mummy (form fitting) kind. These usually have two pounds of down, sometimes three, and are comfortable in temperatures down to 20°.

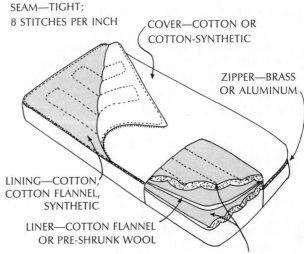

SEAM—TIGHT; 8 STITCHES PER INCH

COVER—COTTON OR COTTON-SYNTHETIC

ZIPPER—BRASS OR ALUMINUM

LINING—COTTON, COTTON FLANNEL, SYNTHETIC

LINER—COTTON FLANNEL OR PRE-SHRUNK WOOL

INSULATION—DOWN OR SYNTHETIC

Synthetic fills. Polyesters, acrylics, or acetates are used almost exclusively in the cheaper sleeping bags now being manufactured. Although their properties are slightly different, all three of these are springy, have a fairly high insulating quality (60 to 70 per cent as efficient as down), do not break up, are insect proof, mildew resistant, and non-allergenic. A well-made bag with 4 pounds of any of these synthetics is adequate in temperatures down to 20-30°. Good liners add up to another 10° of protection. Cost is about $20 to $40, depending on quality.

How much insulation? In most Western states you will want a warm bag, even in summer. In the

CARE OF SLEEPING BAGS

In camp, sleeping bags should be opened and aired several hours daily in good weather. If you are in the forest, string a length of rope between two trees and hang the open bag over it. Or spread the bag over boulders or atop dry grass.

Sleeping bags should be shaken out briskly several times before you retire. This loosens the packed-down insulation and helps you to sleep warmer. Experienced desert campers also shake out bags to remove varmints.

After a trip, sleeping bags can be cleaned some-what by light sponging, but having them dry cleaned by a reputable cleaner is better.

Ideally, when bags are stored at home they should be hung full length, open, and inside out. Most people merely roll them and tuck them away out of sight. You can compromise by taking them out and airing them on the clothesline occasionally. This is essential for down bags, for moths can wreck a valuable bag in a few weeks. Bags should be stored in a dry place, because of the danger of mildew.

Southwest, and most of the remainder of the country, a lighter bag will suffice. During spring and fall months you should have a warm bag almost everywhere except in the deep South.

A sleeping bag is like a big quilt, although the quilted pattern is apt to be one of vertical tubes filled with the insulating material. If these tubes lie parallel with rows of stitching between them, there is no insulation along the stitches. A sleeping bag must retain body heat. These stitched areas allow loss of heat and cut down on the bag's efficiency; this problem is solved by lapping, bonding, or laminating.

Bag linings

These are a matter of personal preference. The material should be durable; good quality cotton, cotton flannel, or any of the synthetics are possible choices. Some people prefer the flannel linings; they seem warmer when you first get into the bag. However flannel linings make it difficult to turn inside your bag. The synthetics retain heat while allowing you to turn easily.

Liners

Removable linings for sleeping bags, or liners, have several advantages: They can make a mediocre bag warmer, they keep the bag interior clean, and they add flexibility to the bag's efficiency under different temperature conditions.

You can make your own liners—light ones of sheeting or cotton flannel, or heavier ones from well-worn blankets.

Construction

Almost all bags today have full length zippers along one side and continuing across the bottom, although some less expensive bags have short zippers reaching only part way down the side. Zippers should be of heavy-duty brass or aluminum. Better bags have flaps covering the zipper on both sides.

What about the stitching? Is the thread heavy, with tight stitches? Are corners bunched? Is the insulation well fixed in place, or will it lump? Test this by taking the bag by the side and shaking it.

Options

Drawings of sleeping bags often show the bag neatly laid out with the little canopy set up to cover the head. You will probably never see one used this way. These flimsy covers would quickly soak through in rain, and only the most hardy camper would remain in his bag in the rain without protection. The flaps do provide a handy wrap-around cover for the rolled bag.

Most sleeping bags have an air mattress pocket in the sleeping bag, but few people bother with them. They are hard to use, and they make the bag difficult to roll.

Some of the better bags have flaps sewn into the top which you can fold down around your shoulders in cold weather.

Air pillows are available. Deflated, they don't take up much space, and some campers like them; you'll need a pillow cover. Most people take old, small pillows, or use a duffel bag or folded clothing beneath the sleeping bag flap.

Hammocks

A camp hammock takes up little space in the car trunk, and once slung between two trees it offers an irresistible attraction to the tired or lazy camper. You can get them in sporting goods stores or government surplus outlets. A new type of nylon net rolls up to about the size of a softball.

Mattresses

A good air mattress can make the difference between a pleasant camping trip and a miserable one. Few campers are hardy enough to sleep on hard ground with comfort, and a cot can be too cold or too narrow to suit many campers. Most campers use air mattresses beneath their sleeping bags—on a cot or on the ground—with or without a ground cloth.

For warmth, the air mattress is usually placed on the ground, on top of a waterproof ground cloth.

Rubberized air mattresses. The better air mattresses are rubberized fabric and rubber. While these cost more than plastic ones, they are considerably more dependable. Cost varies according to the amount of rubber used, the kind of fabric, size, and the quality of manufacturing. Rubberized nylon, or another sturdy material, is probably your best choice. The all-rubber mattresses tend to deteriorate eventually. Don't use a rubberized air mattress as a raft. You will shorten its life by such use, and it may be ruined.

Plastic air mattresses. These mattresses are lightweight, colorful, and inexpensive. Children love them for playing in the water. They are less dependable than rubberized kinds; they are easily punctured by pine needles and sharp stones; they are hard to repair (particularly when the leak is at a seam, corner, or around the inflating tube); and some are defective at time of purchase—blow them up when you get home and let them stand overnight, preferably with some weight on top.

Air mattress pump. Inflation by mouth can be a chore, especially if you are well above sea level and have several mattresses to inflate. If you decide to buy an air mattress pump, try it out first.

Care of your air mattress. Most people leave their air mattresses inflated for the entire period they are camping, and merely pile them in a stack out of the way of foot traffic during the day. Don't overinflate for sleeping; you need just enough air to suspend you.

The mattress should be packed so edges will not rub against one another; seams can be weakened if this occurs.

Foam pads. Some campers and backpackers prefer lightweight foam pads, which need only be unrolled to be ready for sleeping. Some must be protected with a waterproof cover. They come in full and half lengths. Try one out before buying to be certain it is resilient enough for comfort.

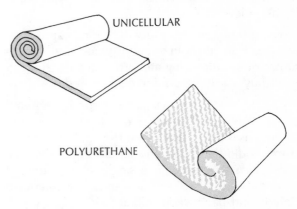

UNICELLULAR

POLYURETHANE

Should you ever find it necessary to get along without a mattress, try the backpacker's trick of making hollows in the ground to fit your hips and shoulders. This allows your spine to remain straight.

Ground cloths

Campers who sleep on the ground use a waterproof ground cloth to protect the sleeping bag from soil moisture and dirt, and to provide additional warmth. Ground cloths aren't necessary for persons sleeping in a tent.

You can buy ground cloths at sporting goods stores in a variety of sizes and materials. The new space-age blankets, an adaptation of the insulation used on space missions, are lightweight, waterproof, and have outstanding insulating qualities. Or you can improvise your own ground cloth from a piece of plastic or waterproofed canvas. A poncho also works fine.

In an emergency a ground cloth can be used for a sleeping shelter or wind break, or for covering supplies. The poncho also makes a raincoat, or paired with another poncho, a pup tent.

Cots

A cot can add to camping comfort, particularly in desert areas where you want to sleep cool (and avoid friendly little critters that roam at night); in cooler areas it can spoil a night's rest. Cots are cold—cool air passes freely underneath the sleeper—unless the cot is well insulated with blankets and plenty of newspapers.

Even with a good bag you must provide insulation between your bag and cot. An air mattress helps solve the problem, or you can use an old blanket doubled over, a folded ground cloth, or several layers of heavy wrapping paper or newspaper. De luxe camp cots are available with built-in insulation.

You'll find a wide variety of folding camp cots, ranging from the old standby wood and canvas army cot to units using modern materials. You can even buy a folding double-decker model.

Check to see that the fabric is strong and well sewn. Too many cots rip out long before the frame has shown any wear. The folding mechanism should be sturdy; you should be able to lock it in place so the cot is a single straight unit. It should be easy to set up, and convenient to handle and pack when folded.

LIGHT AND HEAT

When evening comes, light is needed to continue activities until bedtime.

Flashlights

Good 2 or 3-cell flashlights are a must for every camping trip. You should take along several, preferably one for each member of the group except small children. Carry a supply of extra batteries. Some small lights can be clipped to clothing or to a sleeping bag.

Lanterns

The camper has a wide choice of lanterns manufactured for outdoor use.

Gasoline lanterns. The familiar old gasoline pressure lantern, now redesigned into a more compact shape, is still widely used. It uses white gasoline, which can be purchased in sealed cans in some sporting goods stores. (If you have your own can, you can often buy white gas at supply points near recreational areas, although it is difficult to find elsewhere.) The lantern gives off a brilliant white

CAMPING EQUIPMENT YOU CAN RENT

If you are trying out camping for the first time, or if you prefer to wait awhile before buying equipment, you can fill in the gaps by renting (or borrowing) the items you need for a camping trip. Check your local sporting goods stores, ski shops, camping equipment stores, trailer and boat firms, and general rental organizations to find out what is available.

Renting gives you greater variety and greater flexibility in your equipment. It spares you the bother of storing large items that you might use only once a year. You can try out various types or sizes of gear before buying. Some firms will apply part of the rental fee on purchase.

Rental firms usually specify rates for a 3-day weekend and for the first week; often they will charge a reduced rate for succeeding weeks. Some

firms do not rent for shorter periods than a week.

Rental charges are usually based on the original cost of the item, so you may find equipment offered at a wide range in fees. On smaller or less expensive items, the rental charges are sometimes not much less than the purchase price.

You can usually rent the following equipment: tents of various styles and sizes, sleeping bags, cots, air mattresses, stoves, lanterns, tools, ice chests, camp tables, chairs, and tools.

Some stores feature combination rentals—providing several basic items at a special rate.

If you shop around, you'll find firms renting specialized gear, such as cooking kits, station wagon pads, tent heaters, tarpaulins, ground cloths, fishing tackle, and car-top luggage carriers.

FUEL LANTERNS

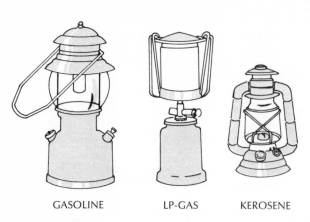

GASOLINE   LP-GAS   KEROSENE

ELECTRIC LANTERNS

ALL-PURPOSE   FLUORESCENT   SWIVEL

light. Gasoline lanterns have built-in pumps to pressurize the fuel.

LP-gas lanterns. A similar lantern burns LP-gas, using replaceable tanks. These are convenient to use—they don't have to be pumped up periodically—but you must carry additional storage tanks. A new model has a refillable LP-gas container with hoses which can be connected to both a stove and lantern; its only drawback is limited portability.

Both the gasoline and LP-gas lanterns use mantles; carry a supply of extra mantles in case you damage those in the lamp.

Electric lanterns. There are dozens of electric lanterns on the market, powered by 6-volt batteries. These appeal to campers who dislike carrying extra fuel. Many of them are all-purpose, but some are concentrated spotlight-only models.

There are good portable units handy to use inside a tent—one you can use for a reading lamp, another is fluorescent and can also be plugged into 110-volt lines.

The 6-volt battery is advertised as good for 100 hours of intermittent use, but if accidentally left on, it will use up the battery in a day. You probably should carry an extra battery or two.

Kerosene lanterns. Some old-timers swear by the old farm-type kerosene lantern. They are dependable and burn a long time on a little fuel; however the kerosene smell bothers some people. Even with caps screwed down tightly, the odor permeates the rest of the load, and spilled fuel enroute is a calamity. When you handle or refill the lantern, the smell seems to cling to your hands through several washings.

We are accustomed to brighter lights, and the soft glow of the old kerosene wick light may seem too dim.

Heaters

You probably won't need heat for camping during the summer months unless you run into a prolonged rainy spell; usually it is more practical for each person to carry an extra sweater or jacket for chilly nights and mornings.

Allow some ventilation in your tent if you use a heater. Not only may they burn up oxygen, but they give off fumes which can cause serious illness or even death.

If you are camping in cold weather, two flameless heaters are now available; an infra-red model

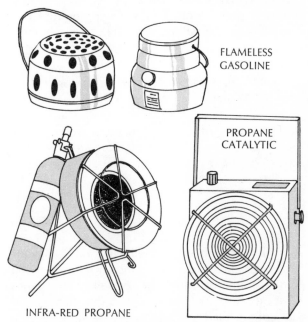

FLAMELESS GASOLINE

PROPANE CATALYTIC

INFRA-RED PROPANE

which can also be used for cooking, and the more common catalytic type which operates on the same principle as sportsmen's handwarmers. Both heaters operate on LP-gas and are recommended as safe either outside or inside.

CAMP TOOLS

You'll need a few basic tools in camp for sprucing up your area, making repairs, cutting or splitting firewood, or cleaning fish. Outside of established campgrounds on federal public lands you are required to carry a shovel and ax.

You may want to paint the handles of your tools a bright color; this makes them easier to locate if misplaced and also identifies them.

Hand ax

If you buy an ax, get a good one, not too light in weight. Recommended specifications: 2½-pound head, with 28-inch handle. The head should have one flat side for hammering. Avoid double-bitted axes—they are extremely dangerous to use when other people are nearby.

The cutting edge of an ax should be kept sharp, and the head should be protected by a sheath at all times when not in use. This prevents the edge from getting nicked or dulled by contact with other metallic surfaces and prevents campers from accidentally wounding themselves.

If kept sharp, the small camp ax used by Boy Scouts is useful around most campgrounds. You can use it for pounding tent stakes, as a hammer, and for making kindling and shavings to start a fire.

Check campground regulations before using your ax. At many campsites you may use "down" wood—that is, dead branches on the ground—but you are not allowed to chop down other vegetation. In heavily-used camping areas you will have to bring your own wood or fuel, or buy it locally.

Saw

A small folding buck saw will cut sizable logs for firewood, and it takes up almost no space when folded. Camping supply stores sell several types of sportsmen's saws with collapsible frames and fast cutting blades. There is even a thin, flexible

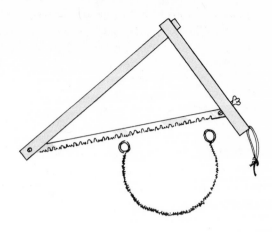

saw with two rings on the end which takes virtually no space at all; to use it you select a green branch with some spring, notch it on the ends, and string the saw like a bow.

Knives

A sheath knife hanging from the belt with a well-sharpened blade will be used many times a day—cutting bait for fishing or rope for a tent stay, shaving wood for kindling, sometimes for slicing food around the campfire. Outdoorsmen find it better than a pocketknife because it is so accessible.

Other campers prefer to carry a good pocketknife; you will find a selection ranging from simple cutting tools to some that are small tool kits. Probably most versatile is the bright red Swiss army knife; different models are available which include a spear blade, can opener, screwdriver, Phillips screwdriver, punch-awl, cap lifter, scissors, saw, and corkscrew. Some campers consider this type of knife a gadget, but it is sturdily made and it is likely to be used many times during a camping trip.

The familiar Boy Scout knife also has an awl and a screwdriver blade.

Fishermen may prefer to carry their own special knives, with a long clip blade for skinning and a toothed blade for scraping.

Shovel

Along with the ax, a shovel is required in undeveloped federal areas. It is used for ditching the tent, digging holes for a latrine, burying garbage, and for shoveling dirt on the fire. The rigid-handled shovels, rather than folding-handled models, are more efficient for straight digging.

Best shovel for camp has a round-point blade and a 30-inch handle; it is adequate for any digging a camper will need to do, and it will fit into the trunk of a passenger car.

Broom

A broom will help to keep the floor of your tent clean, to tidy up the camp, to sweep forest litter off camp tables, and to clean off tents, tarps, and sleeping bags when you roll them up for the trip home. You can use a broom with detachable handle, a child's play broom, or you can shorten the handle of an old household broom. Some campers get along fine with a whisk broom.

Rope

Carry a 100-foot coil of light rope—preferably ¼-inch Manila. If you must cut it, make lengths about 25 feet long, even if they are longer than you presently need.

You can use rope in tying luggage to the car, rigging windbreaks and tarp shelters, for clotheslines, and for hoisting food out of the reach of visiting animals.

Heavy cord. A ball of cord will prove useful in anchoring small tarps or tents, tying bulky parcels, and performing other services around camp.

Work gloves

A pair of ordinary cotton work gloves will protect your hands when you handle fire-blackened pots, pans, grates, and grills. Some campers prefer them to hot pads for handling hot cooking utensils.

COOKING AND DINING EQUIPMENT

In selecting cooking and dining utensils, campers agree on only one thing: keep the assortment simple.

But simplicity means different things to different campers: the vehicle camper tows a complete kitchen into the woods; most car campers carry an ample assortment of utensils and appliances; the veteran backpacker carries a tiny stove, a couple of pots, a cup, plate, and a few utensils in his compact pack. Each of these campers likes to think that he has reduced his cooking and dining equipment to a sensible minimum. Each wants to carry as little as possible while still camping comfortably in his chosen manner.

The style of camping you select will determine much of your equipment; storage, weight, and space considerations are also important.

A wide assortment of equipment is described in the following pages to help you select the items that will make camp cooking and dining an enjoyable experience for you and your family. Utensils that function well not only make the cook's work easier, but mean better camp fare for everybody.

CAMPFIRE COOKING

Learning to build a good wood fire, and keeping its heat output at the temperature you need long enough to do your cooking, is the first principle in campfire cooking.

The right kind of fire is important; most beginning campers make the mistake of building a roaring campfire for cooking, when all that is required is a small, steady fire. A roaring fire has uneven heat, and flames shoot up around the pots and pans blackening them unnecessarily. A fire built of hardwood that has burned down awhile, until it is beginning to form glowing coals, furnishes the steady, even heat needed for cooking.

Most campers in organized campgrounds supplement the wood fire with a portable camp stove, barbecue, or hibachi. These are portable, economical to operate, and provide a faster, more reliable source of heat.

Fire irons

For cooking over an open fire, several pieces of scrap iron can be useful while taking little room. Two or three 18 or 24-inch lengths can be used as pokers, or rested on rocks above a fire to make a utensil rack. A square of sheet metal can be used to prevent utensils from becoming coated with soot. Wrap irons in canvas or newspapers.

STOVES

Almost all auto campers use some version of the folding camp stove. For transport these models fold into a compact, easy-to-handle size. Opened, the back raises and fixes into position, two wings swing out at the sides for further wind protection, and the stove is ready for use in a minute or two.

Most of these camp stoves are two-burner models; a larger three-burner model is also on the market, while backpackers use compact one-burner stoves. Both white gasoline and LP-gas types are available. Prices range from $14 to $40.

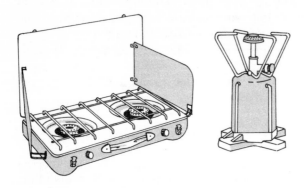

Cooking on these stoves is similar to cooking on a gas stove at home; however burner heat is slower acting and you have less stove-top space. For their size, though, they are very efficient.

Stove accessories

A collapsible stand is available to hold your stove; you can set it up near the fireplace and keep the cooking clutter in one area, away from the dining table. The stands fold down to about 2 feet long, 2 inches per side. Made of lightweight aluminum, they will hold any size stove and cost less than $10.

Collapsible ovens are manufactured for the larger stoves. These set atop one or two burners; you control the temperature by turning the burners up or down; the ovens have temperature indicators.

A toaster-griddle fits across two burners. This is especially popular with the flapjacks-for-breakfast crowd, but you'll find many other uses for it too.

Some models have removable wire grids and grease catchers for cooking bacon.

A camp stove lighter is available which uses ordinary lighter flints.

Fuels

The advent of portable pressurized containers of LP-gas, usually propane but sometimes butane, greatly stimulated camp stove design. A wide assortment of ingenious, lightweight, compact stoves can now be purchased at moderate prices.

Most folding camp stoves now operate on either bottled LP-gas or white gasoline.

When closed, the fuel tank is usually stored inside the stove. In use, the tank attaches to the front, side, or underneath (depending on the model) with a threading connection. When this is disconnected, automatic valves shut off the flow of fuel.

A 6-ounce LP-gas container will fuel one burner at moderate heat for about 3 hours; the larger 14-ounce size lasts about twice as long. Larger refillable containers now on the market will take considerably more. These are rounded containers, about the size of a bowling ball; you get attachments to connect with and fuel both your stove and lantern. (Your lantern will be most handy, however, if you select a model which also can be detached and fueled separately from a smaller cartridge.)

One-burner stoves

The solitary hunter, fisherman, or backpacker finds the one-burner stove provides adequate heat with minimum size and weight. It is seldom sufficient for car campers, except for supplementary cooking. These models are fueled by gasoline, LP-gas, or alcohol. You will find them in stores which specialize in backpacking and mountaineering equipment. Some models nest the burner unit with a couple of pots, frying pan, and wind screen into a compact package weighing only 2 or 3 pounds.

You can also buy an inexpensive one-burner stove fueled by canned jellied gasoline. It has a collapsible frame which takes little space on the camp table.

Barbecue or grill

You may want to take a small table-model barbecue, particularly if you have access to fresh or frozen meat. Operated in conjunction with a stove, your cooking time will be reduced substantially.

Folding camp grills are available in camping supply stores. Some models have folding legs that can be poked into the ground. Camp grills are often sold with a protective bag, because the metal becomes greasy and sooty.

A medium-sized Japanese hibachi is also suitable for grilling.

Remember to carry charcoal briquets and starter liquid with you if they will be needed in camp.

INSULATED CONTAINERS

Ice chests and coolers are excellent for overnight and weekend camping trips, but for use on an extended camping trip you must find a source of ice. The chests also occupy considerable space.

Almost all camp coolers made today use plastic foam insulation. Prices vary widely depending on exterior construction and size.

Inexpensive plastic foam chests are efficient if they have a tight fitting cover. While they are more easily dented and broken, their low price makes it feasible to replace them as needed. They are also much lighter in weight.

To refrigerate foods, precool the chest before placing food supplies in it. Campers do this in several ways: fruit juice frozen in plastic water jugs, solid blocks of ice frozen in clean milk cartons, freezable jell refrigerants, boxes of frozen foods (use within two or three days).

Jugs and bottles. Some campers like to fill a thermos with hot coffee at night so they can have a cup immediately on rising.

POTS AND PANS

Good cooking equipment makes life more pleasant for the camp cook. If you will be cooking on both a standard camp fireplace and a portable camp stove, be certain your equipment is suitable for both.

You want sturdily-made utensils which will take hard camp wear. Make certain the handles are adequate and will stand high heat. You may want to encase soot-blackened pots in cloth sacks (easily made at home from denim).

You can use cooking utensils from home, if you wish, but they may get blackened by wood smoke; aluminum, particularly, is difficult to clean. Campers sometimes rub bar soap liberally over the outside of the pan before use; soot comes off with the soap when the pan is washed. Liquid detergent, wiped on pot bottoms with a paper towel, also does the trick. Others cover the outside of the pan with aluminum foil.

If all of your cooking will be done on a camp stove, lighter-weight pots and pans will conserve fuel, and your heat will be under easy control.

Keep stove size in mind when you buy pots; big pots may not fit on average-sized stoves.

For some campers, space is a consideration. You can buy nested units or you can select the pieces separately and assemble your own compact kit.

Try to apply the nesting principle whenever possible. Pack smaller pots inside large pots, and tuck small packets or odds and ends into open spaces.

Nested cooking sets

Campers' nesting kits are an extension of the smaller, less complicated sets used by backpackers and mountaineers. The small kits are not adequate for family cooking, and they contain a minimum of pieces.

The nesting principle is an intriguing one. Several cooking pots and lids, a frying pan, sometimes a mixing bowl, plates, cups, and eating utensils, fit compactly together into a single lightweight carrying unit. More expensive kits may have heat-resistant pot handles (some which detach for packing) or nonstick finishes on cooking surfaces.

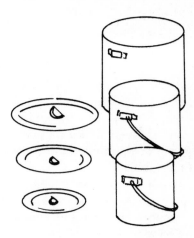

Camp supply stores offer a choice of sets ranging from small 2-man and 4-man kits to outfits for a large group.

Some kits now contain melamine plates and cups instead of metal ones. This is particularly important when drinking hot liquids; metal cups often result in burned lips.

Lightweight units which use pot lids as frying pans are often difficult to use. The small size and straight sides hamper the cook, while pans without handles are hard to use over a hot fire. Aluminum cannot be used over a very hot fire, as it heats

COOKING POTS heat on grill over simple rock-lined fireplace. Nesting pots have bail handles.

STURDY GRIDDLE of heavy aluminum or cast-iron turns out pancakes, bacon, and eggs for hungry campers.

too rapidly and foods may burn and stick. Stainless steel pots conduct a more even heat.

Flat-topped kettles with covers and bail handles telescope readily and can be stacked one on top of the other to keep food warm.

Frying pan

A heavy cast iron frying pan with a metal handle is almost a must for cooking over a wood fire. You can cook a wide variety of foods—in large quantities—in it, and campers find it particularly useful on the conventional campground fireplace grill.

You can take along a frying pan from home, or, if you prefer not to get your kitchenware sooty, you can buy one just for camping. If space and weight are important, steel and aluminum pans with folding handles are available.

Popular sizes are 8 and 9 inches in diameter; larger skillets can be obtained for big groups.

Some campers who do a lot of fishing take a separate skillet for frying fish so that no fish flavor intrudes on other fried foods.

Griddle

A griddle will enable you to dole out bacon, eggs, and pancakes in quantity. Sizes and materials vary; but the heavier the metal, the better pancakes turn out.

Since the griddle becomes sooty after use, you'll want to wrap it in newspapers or a cloth bag.

Coffeepot

The capacious old-timers' enameled pot is still found in hardware and camp supply stores. You can buy pots with capacity up to 5 quarts. Your home coffee pot may serve if you don't mind a little smudging.

Saucepans

Take along at least 2 saucepans. Depending on the size of your group, the smaller pan should be 1 to 3-quart size, the larger 2 to 5-quart size. If you buy them strictly for camping use, look for the squatty, flat-bottomed and flat-topped varieties.

Pressure cooker

Optional. If you plan to camp in high altitudes, a pressure cooker cuts meal preparation time considerably. You can also use it for one-dish meals.

Reflector oven

Usable only in undeveloped camping areas. You need a real campfire to use a reflector oven; they allow you to bake biscuits, bread, pies, and cakes, or to broil fish, meat, and bacon by reflected heat. The polished aluminum parts fold into a slim, flat package for transport. The oven should be stable enough to be picked up and moved.

Dutch oven

Usable only in undeveloped camping areas. The outdoorsman's sturdy, 3-legged pot is set above coals for long, slow cooking, and more coals are heaped on the pot's slightly concave cover. Heavy-duty cast iron containers weigh from 12 to 35 pounds, depending on size. The Dutch oven can be used for stewing, braising, and baking.

Water bucket

A 2-gallon bucket or a large 5-gallon can is needed for hauling and heating water for dishes, cooking, and washing. Although bulky, these containers can be packed with gear for transporting to camp.

Canvas buckets take less space, but they cannot be used for heating water.

COOKING UTENSILS AND SUPPLIES

Standard cooking tools are useful on a camping trip. You may want to add your own favorites.

Can opener
Beer-can opener
Kitchen knife (protect blade with sheath)
Paring knife
Vegetable peeler
2 large mixing spoons
Pancake turner or spatula
Cooking fork (stick tines in cork)
Toasting rack (either long-handled or stove-top)
Potato masher
Egg beater or whisk
Measuring spoons
Mixing bowls
Salt and pepper set (should be moisture-proof)
Tongs for picking up hot vegetables, pots
Knife sharpener
The following paper and foil products are useful:
Clear plastic film or waxed paper
Aluminum foil
Paper bags
Plastic bags in several sizes; twist ties
Paper towels
Disposable aluminum foil pans

DINING EQUIPMENT

Each camper should have his own plate, bowl, cup, and silverware. You can mark names with a felt-tip marker.

Plates

Camping dinnerware should be durable—it must withstand rough handling and be immersible in hot water. Inexpensive, unbreakable melamine ware, usually available in open stock, is a good choice which lasts through many camping trips.

Compartmented plates are popular for camping; they organize the dinner and prevent foods from running together on the plate.

You can also find other durable plates in aluminum, enamelware, and heavy china. Light plastic picnic plates are not sturdy enough for camping.

Disposable plates. Most campers take along a few paper plates, mainly for meals that require no cooking. Some campers save compartmented trays from frozen TV dinners for use in camp.

You can buy compartmented paper plates; some are made to fit inside supporting metal trays.

Bowls

A bowl or deep-rimmed pie tin can be used for cereal, soup, stewed fruit, and pudding.

Cups

Don't buy aluminum or tin cups; when filled with a hot beverage they burn the lips. Heavy plastic is best; double-walled ones hold heat better. Some campers prefer enamelware cups or china mugs.

Disposable cups. Plastic coated cups, which fit into plastic holders and pressed urethane foam cups are also good for hot liquids.

Cutlery

Inexpensive stainless steel knives, forks, and spoons are ideal for camping. Avoid sets with plastic handles; they might become damaged in the campfire or in scalding dishwater. For camp health, sterilize commonly-shared cutlery and cups every two or three days by boiling.

TABLES

An auxiliary table comes in handy in a campground; you can use it for your food preparation area, leaving the permanent table and benches for sitting and eating. Your food storage box can be placed at one side, leaving ample work room.

Folding camp tables are available which compact into the size of a small card table. You can also buy a folding unit which opens into a table and two benches, which is intended primarily for dining.

DISHWASHING AND CLEANUP

Dishwashing requirements are also similar to those at home:

- 2 dishpans, nesting (can heat water in metal ones)
- Soap or detergent
- Dish mop or cloth
- Steel wool or scouring pads
- Cleanser
- Vegetable brush
- Dish towels
- Dish drainer
- Rags
- Plastic garbage bags
- Length of clothesline
- Handful of clothespins

MEDICINE CABINET hangs on tree. It has mirror, holds medical, health supplies. Lid folds and locks to pack.

BATHROOM CENTER

While you probably won't be able to keep quite as clean as you can at home, certain amenities must still be met. You can assemble your toilet articles in a small space in a camp bathroom and washing center; the first aid kit and medicines belong here, too.

Toilet articles

Each person should be responsible for his own personal toilet articles. Also bring toothpaste, nail clippers, disposable tissues, medicines.

Soap

Carry bath-sized bar soap. Removed from the wrapper ahead of time, it will harden and last longer. To prevent loss of soap, buy a floating type or drill a hole through the cake and run a cord through it; you can hang it from a tree branch or around your neck.

A large tube of lather shaving cream is a handy substitute for bar soap and shampoo; it is less likely to slip out of your hands and disappear in the stream.

You may want some hard water soap for washing out clothing.

Towels

Take dark colored towels which will not show the dirt. Plan on two towels per camper. You can save your old bath towels for camp and then discard them when vacation is over.

Wash basin

For those who prefer not to use one of the dishpans as a wash basin, there are basins of tin, plastic, and canvas available. The canvas basin collapses into a flat disc.

Mirror

A brightly polished metal mirror is best for camping because it cannot be broken, and it can be carried in a hiker's pocket for use as a distress signal. Heavy plate glass camp mirrors are also available.

Toilet paper

Although furnished in most organized camp-grounds, it's safer to take some along. Coffee cans or plastic bags make good waterproof containers.

Hot water bottle

Optional. A hot water bottle is useful for warming cold feet and cramped muscles. (Cold feet can also be warmed with a canteen filled with hot water or a hot rock wrapped in newspapers and toweling.)

First aid kit

The average prepared first aid kit is inadequate for an extended camping trip. Illness or injury can be frightening in a remote camp. Yet it is pointless to carry equipment you don't know how to use.

If you want to make up your own kit, here is a list of items to consider:

2 triangular bandages
Band-aids
Gauze pads
2-inch adhesive tape
Elastic bandages (for strains)
Spray antiseptic, iodine, or tincture of
    Merthiolate
Scissors
Safety pins
Cotton
Aspirin
Bicarbonate of soda (for indigestion, burns,
    insect bites)
Chapstick
Antiseptic surgical powder
Suntan oil or lotion (sun screen type)
Burn ointment
Poison oak lotion
Disinfectant soap
Vaseline
Fingernail brush
Tweezers (for splinters)
Magnifying glass (for finding splinters)
Needles (for removing splinters)
Salt tablets (to prevent heat exhaustion)
Snake bite kit
Chlorine or Halazone tablets (to purify water)
Spirits of ammonia ampules (for faintness)
Laxative (especially for mountain camping)
Pectin medicine (for diarrhea)

Boric acid powder (for chafing, eye wash)
Chewing gum (for ears in high altitudes)
Toothache remedy
Eyecup (metal)
Antihistamine for insect bite reactions
Prescription medicine to kill pain
Prescription sedative
First aid handbook

RECREATION

Half the fun of camping is surviving—providing wood, water, food, and shelter—and fixing up the campsite to make it more comfortable. Other pastimes depend on the site and your interests: hiking, fishing, swimming, or just loafing, sun-bathing, and reading.

A plastic air mattress or one-man life raft is fun for youngsters in shallow water. Adults can also use it for lazy floating in quiet water or as a boat for lake fishing.

Guide books on trees, wildflowers, wildlife, and geology will help you know your surroundings better.

Small children will want to bring crayons, col-oring books, and a few favorite small toys for quiet time in camp. But set a reasonable limit. You may want to make each child a colorful 12-inch-square drawstring bag for his possessions—and make that the limit. Some families enjoy outdoor craft projects.

Hobby equipment

You will want to bring along equipment for any sports or hobbies you plan to pursue. You may want your camera and accessories, binoculars, fishing tackle, water-skis, or other equipment. If you are camping near gold country, you may want to try gold panning (gold pans can be bought in small-town general stores in the area). If you like campfire songfests and won't disturb other camp-ers, bring a guitar or harmonica and perhaps a songbook or two.

Rainy day activities

Pack a few items to bring out on the rainy day when everyone is confined to camp, or for the

CAMP BOX

A fishing tackle box makes a good container for keeping small tools and miscellaneous items in one handy place.

Pliers. You can use these to pick up hot pots and pans, remove foil-wrapped foods from the fire, tighten wing nuts on camp equipment, and cut wire. Sportsmen's pliers, with a wire cutter on the side, are particularly useful.

Hammer. If you expect to build some of your camp facilities on the spot, this will be less awkward than using the ax.

Nails. A few nails of assorted sizes can be used for camp repairs. Don't drive nails into trees.

Coil of wire. A small coil or spool of light wire (9 gauge) can be used for repairing equipment, improvising handles and hooks.

Candles. A few stubs will provide emergency light and help start a fire after a rain.

Tent repair kit. You need scraps of canvas, a tube of canvas adhesive, a heavy sail needle, and a spool of heavy thread for canvas repairs.

Sewing kit. A small kit containing needles, thread, buttons, and a zipper repair kit.

Air mattress repair kit

Extra shoe laces

One-inch adhesive tape

Safety pins

Small notebook and pencil

Friction tape

---

lazy day when everyone prefers to stay in camp and relax. Here are a few suggestions:

Playing cards
Checkers, chess, cribbage board (you can buy combination boards or small travelers' sets)
Crossword puzzle books
Nature books (trees, flowers, birds, etc.)
Paperback books and magazines

MISCELLANEOUS ITEMS

A few items are hard to classify or overlap several categories.

Newspapers

A bundle of newspapers has a number of uses in camp: to cover the tent floor to protect it from tracked-in dirt, as insulation under an air mattress, for disposal of garbage and fish cleanings, to start the campfire. If you don't use your entire stack, give the remainder to a nearby camper.

Mosquito netting

Sometimes you'll find mosquitoes in hordes, particularly near quiet lakes or where soggy breeding places exist; you may want to pack netting as a precaution. Durable nylon or cotton netting may be purchased in fine or medium mesh. You can

buy it formed into a canopy to suspend over a cot, and also in the shape of a hood to wear over your head. You can also drape mosquito netting over your food to protect against flies.

Insect repellent

Insect pests bother the camper in two ways: flying pests which attack him in person, and crawling pests which wander into the tent or the food. Protection has two phases, personal and campsite.

Personal insect repellents are obtainable in liquid, spray, or stick forms. Some types are effective for some individuals and not for others. You may want to try several kinds to see which one works the best for you.

Some campers take spray repellents with them and spray the area and the tent before retiring (don't go to bed while the vapor is still lingering). Ant powder will keep those pests away from your food supply. Repellents are available which burn and give off smoke that is unpleasant to insects, but often it is none too pleasant for campers either.

Camp chairs

If you have room to carry them, you may want to take along some folding chairs. Tired campers find them more comfortable than sitting on the ground or on logs or benches.

Camp clock

You may want to leave your good watches home and rely on a cheap alarm clock. Your interest in exact time of day is pretty casual, but a clock comes in handy in some circumstances.

CAMP CLOTHING

The clothes you need for camping are similar to the ones you wear for gardening or weekend loafing at home. Nearly every item is probably already hanging in your closet or folded in a dresser.

In general, camp clothing should be light in weight, comfortable and practical, and fashioned from fabrics that do not show dirt, are easy to wash, and are not likely to snag or tear. The experienced camper chooses clothes that will protect him in any weather, and he keeps his needs simple. Beginners often take more than they need.

Children's clothes should be washable or expendable, and should be taken in sufficient quantity for frequent changes. Provide extra warmth and good sun protection for them; children often feel cold more intensely than do adults, and they are more sensitive to exposure to sunlight.

Shirts. For the men, take along sweat shirts and plenty of T-shirts. Women will need sturdy, non-iron dark-colored cotton shirts. Wool shirts may be needed for evening or for a cold snap, but they usually are too warm for daytime camping wear.

T-shirts and sweat shirts make ideal wear for children. One family puts aside the children's shirts when they reach the one-more-wear stage and takes the year's accumulation to camp. After the children finish wearing them, the shirts are either used as cleaning rags or discarded.

Pants. Typical work pants—grays, tans, and jeans—are the standard camp uniform for men. Many women prefer slacks to jeans, although the latter are sturdier and will take rougher treatment. Denim frontier pants are another practical choice.

Shorts or culottes are fine for wear in camp or for hiking along well-defined trails, but they offer no protection in rough country.

For safety, remove the cuffs from long pants. They may catch on exposed roots, twigs, and rocks.

Underwear. Your usual wear; in high altitudes you may want thermal underwear.

Shoes. Loafers and oxfords are comfortable in camp—although they pick up small pebbles and pine needles—but they do not provide either enough support or protection for long hikes. Non-skid-soled work boots make a fine camp shoe.

Take along an extra pair of shoes in case one pair gets soaked. Worn-out tennis shoes are good for wading through pebbly streams.

Children will usually wear tennis shoes or sneakers. High-topped ones are better for keeping out stones and dirt, and they give better ankle support and protection.

Socks. Knit synthetics or heavy knitted cotton socks are good, preferably athletic socks. Wool doesn't wear well and shrinks badly.

Sleepwear. Campers sleep in almost anything—underwear, pajamas, clothes—depending on the night temperature. Cotton flannel pajamas are fine if you do not wear them in a bag lined with the same material; the two flannel surfaces stick together as if glued. Socks will keep feet warm.

Some campers consider long-legged gym suits—sweat shirts and sweat pants—an ideal type of camp sleepwear. You can wear the suit around camp in the morning when you first get up without feeling conspicuous.

For small children, include a favorite blanket to make them feel at home in the wilds.

Headwear. A hat or visored cap will shield your head from sun and rain and can serve even as an emergency water carrier. Give it several coats of waterproof spray. Bandannas have multiple uses—as handkerchief, neck scarf, bandage, hat.

Dress-up. If you think you may get tired of camp fare and eat in a restaurant occasionally, pack one set—and only one—of appropriate clothing for each member of the family.

For rainy weather. Carry emergency protection for everyone—slickers, plastic raincoats, or ponchos. Take along a waterproof hat for each person.

For cold weather. Insulate with layers—a sweater or two plus a windbreaker is usually warmer than a single garment, even a lined one. You may want a warm cap and gloves.

Transporting your equipment

Each year when you finally assemble everything for your camping trip—sleeping bags, tent, tarps, cooking utensils, food, and miscellaneous gear—you wonder how you will be able to transport the mountainous assortment and campers, too.

WEIGHT CONSIDERATIONS

Weight must be considered as well as space. A light car which handles easily with one person in it is comparatively sluggish when you add several hundred pounds of equipment and several more people. Leave marginal items at home. If you are carrying heavy loads, you may need overload springs.

ORGANIZE EQUIPMENT and supplies before you start to pack. Numbers show where equipment goes.

Weight distribution. Most of the load weight should be distributed between the axles. Too much weight behind the rear axle adds strain to the rear springs and shocks, affects the car's steering and headlights.

Weight should be distributed horizontally for easier driving. Unequal distribution—too much weight over one wheel or one side—makes the car sway and steer poorly. Heaviest items go in first, lightest items on top or in a roof-top carrier.

In loading two-wheeled trailers, heaviest items should be forward and low over the axle, to keep the tongue down firmly on the hitch.

How to pack

As every experienced camper knows, there's a trick to packing. Start with a permanent list of supplies, and check them off as you pack. Organize for weight and space as you pack; decide what items go inside with the passengers, what should be placed in the trunk, and what goes into a roof-top carrier or auxiliary trailer.

Camp clothing can be packed in duffel bags or cartons, since wrinkling is unimportant. One flat suitcase should hold the family's one set of good clothes. Stuff small items into boots and shoes; these can be tucked into small spaces or crevices.

Pack food supplies in cardboard boxes or wood containers you make yourself. Square or rectangular containers pack with little waste space. Polyethylene freezer containers are excellent for camping supplies; they are lightweight, nearly airtight, unbreakable, and insect proof.

Place the tent and sleeping bags on the floor of the back seat for best weight distribution. Light gear can go on the car's rear shelf.

Loading the car. When you are ready to load, get EVERYTHING out and around the car before you begin, using your check-off list. You can then select weights and sizes progressively.

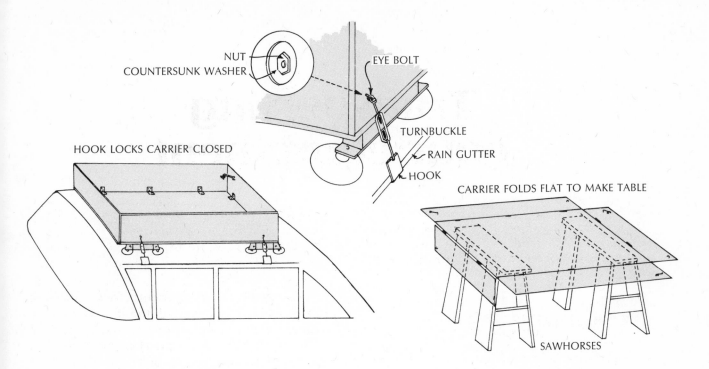

NUT
COUNTERSUNK WASHER

EYE BOLT

HOOK LOCKS CARRIER CLOSED

TURNBUCKLE

RAIN GUTTER

HOOK

CARRIER FOLDS FLAT TO MAKE TABLE

SAWHORSES

CAR-TOP CARRIERS

A roof-top carrier for your car can give you as much extra luggage space as a small trailer, but you should use it only for lightweight items.

High or bulky loads may cause noticeable wind resistance, however, and too heavy a load can affect the car's ease of handling. Extended use of a carrier may mar or discolor the car's finish.

Sports car and convertible owners may want a small carrier that sits on the trunk. It holds less than a roof carrier, but is fine for light items. Other carriers are made especially for convertibles.

Some boat carriers have special loading devices to help swing the boat atop the car. Special carriers are made for skiers, campers, and fishermen.

Making your own carrier. You may want to purchase a set of carrier bars and make your own plywood carrier to ride on them.

In the carrier illustrated above, the sides of the box are hinged and hooked securely in place. A canvas cover is lashed over the box for travel. In camp, the corner hooks are unfastened and the hinged sides fold down to form a flat table. Take-apart sawhorses make the supporting frame.

Coverings should be made of strong material and be large enough to cover the load adequately. Lashings should be of lightweight rope, such as ¼-inch Manila.

Rentals. You can rent a carrier with an inside frame and a cover to protect its cargo for about $5 a week. Camping families find these useful for carrying lightweight, bulky items.

Generally they come in three sizes: A 12-cubic-foot size for imported cars and compacts; a 16-cubic-foot size for larger sedans, and a 24-cubic-foot size for station wagons.

UTILITY TRAILERS

You should be able to rent a lightweight two-wheeled trailer with a box body for about $15-$20 a week. Some of them have lightweight metal or fiberglass covers. Most of these small trailers are rated at ½ ton, which may be larger than you need. While cubic space of the interior may be less than that of a large car-top carrier, the trailer's low center of gravity allows you to pile some of your load above the box and lash a cover over it.

Check to see if insurance on the vehicle is included in the rental fee, and ask your insurance agent if your car insurance covers the contents.

A few single-wheeled trailers are still sold, or you can find an inexpensive used one to buy; they are rarely offered for rent. This trailer is usually a small, ¼-ton box model with a single swiveling wheel mounted centrally beneath the body, and a yoke arrangement which attaches to the car bumper at two points instead of with a pivoting tongue hitch.

Camp cookery

With the variety of cooking equipment and easy-to-prepare foods now on the market, camp cooking can be as simple or as elaborate as you want it.

Vehicle camper cooks can prepare meals similarly to the way they do at home. Backpackers, however, will rely heavily on dehydrated foods and prepared mixes, with a minimum of equipment. Car campers within easy distance of food stores find pre-planning less important; those far from supplies must plan and shop carefully.

WHAT'S SPECIAL ABOUT CAMP COOKING?

There are, however, some significant, if subtle, differences between home and camp cooking, and these differences affect your shopping list.

CAMPFIRE COOKING is not difficult if you carry the right equipment. Use quick and simple recipes.

Not all of these principles will apply in all camping situations, of course. Some camp cooks delight in preparing complicated recipes in a wilderness kitchen. But you can keep these principles in mind as you plan menus and prepare shopping lists.

Easy to prepare. Most cooks prepare simple recipes in camp. Facilities are limited, and no camper wants to spend all vacation as a cook.

Short cooking time. Recipes should be quick cooking. Some foods will take twice as long to cook at high altitudes as they do at sea level.

Limited refrigeration. Foods should keep well with little or no refrigeration. Iceboxes are fine if you are camped near an ice supply; but most of your foods will be canned, dried, freeze-dried, or dehydrated, with a minimum of perishables.

Larger quantities. You eat more when you live outdoors. Exercise and fresh air stimulate appetites, so prepare about 1/3 more than at home.

Limited bulk and weight. Some campers must limit the weight and space of their food supplies. The dehydrated, dried, and freeze-dried foods now on the market will help cut down on both.

Snacks are important. Snack-type foods are nibbled continually in camp and on the trail.

PLANNING CAMP MENUS

Planning camp menus is not complicated. Breakfasts and lunches may be similar to what you have at home; dinner menus will be your main food planning.

Breakfast menus

Hearty breakfasts are essential in camp to fortify you for the active day ahead.

NEW IDEAS FOR CAMP BREAKFASTS

Vary your breakfasts in camp by trying eggs a new way, or by adding fresh or wild fruit to your pancake batter.

Versatile biscuit mix can be used for pancakes, or for coffee cake or hot breakfast rolls by adding jam, nuts, or cinnamon.

To toast bread slices or English muffin halves, pan fry, uncovered, in a small amount of margarine over medium-high heat, until nicely browned on both sides.

Scrambled Eggs with Salmon

Drain 1 can (about 8 oz.) salmon; bone if you wish. In frying pan melt 4 tablespoons margarine and add salmon; heat through. Beat 6 to 8 eggs with a fork until smooth; turn into pan with salmon. Add salt and pepper, and cook slowly, stirring to allow uncooked egg to flow to bottom of pan, until eggs are set. Makes 4 servings.

Creole Eggs and Shrimp

This colorful dish can be served for any meal of the day. For breakfast, you may want to double the number of eggs and adjust the seasonings.

In a medium-sized frying pan, melt 4 tablespoons margarine; add 2 tablespoons chopped onion and sauté until golden. Add 1 can (4½ oz.) shrimp, drained and rinsed, and 2 tablespoons sliced, stuffed green olives; heat through, stirring. Add 2 eggs, slightly beaten, with ¼ teaspoon salt and a dash of pepper. Cook slowly until eggs are set, stirring occasionally. Makes 2 servings.

Eggs Rancheros

In a large frying pan, heat 1 can (10 oz.) enchilada sauce, adding 2 tablespoons dried bell pepper, if desired. Carefully break 4 eggs, one at a time, into the bubbling sauce. Cover pan, set to the side over lower heat, and cook until the eggs are set. Meanwhile, split and toast 2 English muffins. Place one muffin half in each bowl, top with an egg. Spoon over sauce. Makes 4 servings.

Easy Huevos Rancheros

Here's another version of this popular dish.

Put 1 tablespoon margarine in frying pan over heat. Add 2 tablespoons minced onion, 1 can (8 oz.) tomato sauce, 1 minced canned green chile, and about ½ cup cubed jack or Cheddar cheese. Heat until cheese is melted. Break 4 to 6 eggs into this mixture (as for poaching), cover, and cook gently until eggs are set. Makes 2 to 3 servings.

Corned Beef Hash with Eggs

Melt about 2 tablespoons margarine in a heavy frying pan. Crumble into pan 2 cans (15 oz. each) corned beef hash. Stir and heat, then spread mixture in an even layer. Make 6 depressions in the hash with the back of a spoon. Break an egg into each depression, dot with margarine, and sprinkle with salt and pepper. Cover pan; steam slowly 15 minutes, or until eggs are set. Makes 6 servings.

Fried Breakfast Sandwich

Prepare this mixture at home and keep it in the ice chest. The sandwich is assembled in camp.

At home, fry 6 slices bacon until crisp; drain and chop. Mince 3 hard-cooked eggs and ¼ medium-sized green pepper. Put bacon, eggs, and green pepper in a bowl, and add 2 tablespoons minced onion, 1 teaspoon dry mustard, ¼ cup mayonnaise, and salt and pepper to taste; mix well. Refrigerate at home or in ice chest.

In camp, butter 1 side of 2 slices of sandwich bread for each serving. On the unbuttered side of one slice, spread ¼ of the bacon-egg mixture, about ⅓-inch thick; top with the other slice of bread. Cook in a lightly greased frying pan long enough to brown each side and heat through. Makes enough filling for 4 sandwiches.

Cinnamon Toast

Cut bread slices diagonally. Fry slowly in margarine (use about 1 teaspoon margarine for each piece) until golden brown on both sides. Take slices from griddle; drop in paper bag containing 1 cup powdered sugar mixed with 1 tablespoon cinnamon. Shake gently until toast is sugared.

Caramelized Toast

In a shallow pan or bowl, mix 1 cup powdered sugar and 1 tablespoon cinnamon. Stir in about 3 tablespoons water to make a thin paste. Dip slices of French bread in the paste, then fry slowly on both sides in a generous amount of margarine until the bread is golden brown.

COOKING AT HIGH ALTITUDES

If you will be camping in the mountains, the change in atmospheric pressure at higher altitudes will influence your cooking. Foods need more cooking liquid and longer simmering times, and your favorite baking recipes will no longer be foolproof.

Boiling point of water drops about 2° for each 1,000 foot rise in altitude. Any foods which are boiled or steam-cooked get less heat and need longer cooking times than at sea level. You may need to add additional water; rice, for instance, needs more liquid. Poaching is an excellent method of cooking to combat the drying effect of high altitude cooking.

Frozen vegetables cook more quickly than the corresponding fresh ones because they have been blanched before freezing. Solidly packed frozen vegetables should be partially thawed before cooking.

Most fresh vegetables require longer steam-cooking at high altitudes; beets and onions require the longest increase in time.

Baking time for vegetables does not vary with a change in altitude.

Many prepared baking mixes have high altitude cooking directions on the package. If you will be baking cakes in the mountains, you may want to consult a basic or high altitude cookbook to learn the necessary adjustments.

Pressure saucepan cookery. The pressure saucepan is a boon at high altitudes. Increased pressure raises the temperature inside the pan and causes food to cook more rapidly.

Vegetables which must be boiled a long time at high altitudes are far superior in flavor and color if cooked in a pressure saucepan.

Above 3,000 feet even in a pressure cooker you will need to cook whole vegetables, some meats, and meat soup stocks longer than normal.

Breakfast menus are planned around combinations of these items:

1. Fruit—fresh, canned, stewed, or juice
2. Eggs and bacon, ham, sausage, canned or freeze-dried meat
3. Pancakes, toast, biscuits, cornbread, potatoes, or cereal
4. Hot beverage—coffee, tea, or cocoa

Lunch menus

For practical reasons, the camp lunch is usually a cold one. Often some of the party is off fishing or hiking, with lunch in a knapsack.

Lunch menus are planned around these items:

1. Sandwiches (a high-protein filling keeps the camper going until dinner)
2. Sweets—fruits, cookies, or candy
3. Snacks—nuts, carrot sticks, cheese, beef jerky, bacon bars
4. Beverage

Dinner menus

Dinner is usually the main meal, and you have a greater choice of foods and cooking methods.

Camp dinners are usually centered on a main dish (combining meat, starch and vegetable—served separately or stirred together into a one-dish meal) preceded by soup and followed by a salad, if available, and dessert.

You can plan dinner menus around combinations of these items:

1. Soup
2. Meat, fish, or poultry — dried, canned, or freeze-dried
3. Potatoes, pasta, or rice
4. Vegetable — fresh, canned, or dehydrated
5. Salad (if available)
6. Dessert
7. Beverage

Estimating food supplies

If you are relatively inexperienced, plan detailed daily menus and estimate food amounts as closely as you can. As you gain experience, the job gets easier.

1. Start by planning menus for each breakfast and dinner, day by day. Beside each item, list the basic ingredients. Put staple items in a separate column.

If you will not have refrigeration, plan to use perishable items in the first days' menus. Then select canned, dried, and dehydrated foods in their place for later menus.

2. Lunch menus are less rigid, and will depend to some extent on whether they will be eaten in camp or on the trail. It's easiest to list appropriate lunch foods under the following categories: bread and crackers, fillings and spreads; dried meats; fresh and dried fruits; cookies and candy; nuts; and cheese. Make a tentative list of specific items under these categories, based on a rough estimate of the total amounts your family will use. Be sure to allow for between-meal snacks.

3. After each item on your breakfast and dinner menus, estimate the amount per person, adding ⅓ more than normal for increased outdoor appetites, and multiply the individual amount by the number of people to get the total amount needed.

4. After completing your list of breakfast and dinner ingredients, plus lunch supplies, go over the list to identify additional ingredients you will need for preparing, cooking, and flavoring the dishes. These will include margarine, seasonings, sauces, gravies, jam or syrup, dehydrated eggs, and any additional meat, vegetables, or fruit you plan to add to a particular dish. Add them to your list and estimate the amount for each.

Remember to list the beverages you plan to take along, and estimate amounts needed. Double-check your list for any staples you may have omitted. A food check list can be found on page 57.

GROCERY SHOPPING

Now that you have made a list of tentative menus for your camping meals, you are ready to shop. Your menus may undergo some changes during shopping; you may find new items you prefer to substitute.

If you will be camping more than two or three days, you may want to shop in several stores. Start with your favorite supermarket or grocery store; many of its items fit into camp meals. You may also want to explore camp supply stores, health food stores, and delicatessens.

Following are some available foods to consider in your menu planning and shopping.

BREAKFAST

Most of these supplies are standard items that can be purchased at home or in rural grocery stores.

BREAKFAST ON THE TRAIL

These breakfast recipes are handy for backpackers, but can also be used by car campers.

Swiss-Style Cereal

At home, spread 1 cup whole filberts on one baking sheet and 1 cup whole blanched almonds on another. Bake nuts in a 350° oven for 5 to 8 minutes or until very lightly browned; shake pans occasionally. Let nuts cool. Rub filberts between hands to remove as much of brown skin as possible; blow off chaff. Chop nuts coarsely, and blend with 3 cups quick-cooking rolled oats, ¾ cup sweetened wheat germ, 1 cup dried currants, ⅔ cup finely chopped dried apricots, and ¾ cup firmly packed brown sugar. Package in 12 individual plastic bags, ¾ cup per bag. Cereal is ready to serve (no cooking needed) in bowls with milk or reconstituted dried milk. Top with fruit, if you like. Makes 12 servings of ¾ cup size.

Rice Cereal with Apricots

At home, measure into a large, heavy plastic bag ½ teaspoon salt, 1 cup low-fat dry milk product (made with cream), ½ cup rice cereal (for making hot rice cereal), and ¼ cup brown sugar. Seal in a smaller bag ½ cup chopped dried apricots, and add to contents of large bag. Seal package with these cooking instructions:

Combine apricots with 3 cups water, and bring to a boil, covered. Stir in the rice cereal mixture and cook, stirring, at a boil for 1 minute. Cover, remove from heat, and let stand 3 minutes. Makes 4 servings.

Muffin Bread

At home, empty 1 package muffin mix into a plastic bag. Seal bag with mixing directions on box and these cooking instructions:

In camp, grease two large foil pie pans lightly with salad oil. Mix muffin batter according to package directions. Pour batter into one pan, cover with the other pan, and secure with four or five clothespins. Find a spot on the stove top where the heat is low. Bake about 10 minutes, turn pan over using clothespins as handles, and bake about 10 minutes on other side. Remove the top pan, cut in 6 to 8 pieces, and serve with margarine. Makes 6 to 8 servings.

Fruit

Fruits are an essential, healthful part of camp diet because they supply needed vitamins and minerals and provide a tasty contrast to one-pot or skillet camp cookery. They also help satisfy the craving for sweets.

Fresh fruit. Unless you are camping near a store, you will probably be able to count on fresh fruit for only a few days in camp. In mountain or desert air, fresh fruits dry out rapidly; oranges, grapefruit, lemons, apples, pears, and melons survive better than "softer" fruits without refrigeration. Bananas, apricots, and tomatoes can be bought green and allowed to ripen.

Dehydrated fruits. These are a boon to campers. They take up little space and when simmered with water and sugar are easily converted to flavorsome desserts or breakfast appetizers. Some can be eaten as is and make fine trail food.

Packaged applesauce (tiny cubes of quick-cooking apples) is a camper favorite. Also available are dried prunes, dates, apricots, bananas, pears, pineapple, peaches, figs, and mixed fruits which have been cut into small pieces for cooking. Camping supply stores carry packaged fruit slices with sugar added—apricot, peach, apple, and pear. Date nuggets and banana chips are also available.

You can cook the fruit over the coals while you are cleaning up the dinner or breakfast pots and

---

COOKING IN A TRAILER OR CAMPER

If you're the one who does the cooking aboard your trailer or camper, you have much in common with other mobile cooks. You probably work with a small sink, use either a refrigerator or ice box, have well planned storage space—and little or no counter space. You need to keep a ship-shape kitchen in order to work efficiently. And all food and equipment must be packed and stored to ride well in a moving vehicle.

Individual preferences vary widely in the choice of equipment for this kind of cooking. Some people who have camped in tents use their camping cookware exclusively. But the four most generally favored utensils are the Dutch oven, double boiler, frying pan, and pressure cooker. A whistling teapot is another useful item, and many mobile cooks carry a campstove, portable barbecue, or hibachi for greater variety in their menus.

In smaller pieces of kitchen equipment, the simple and the multipurpose ones are most mentioned: a good sharp knife, a cooking spoon and fork, a can opener, and a punch-type opener.

Planning and packing. The planning you do for mobile cooking resembles that for a pack trip—you don't want to carry unnecessary extras, but you do want to eat well. At least the first few times, it helps to plan in detail all that you'll need. One mobile cook keeps two permanent but flexible lists, one for utensils, one for food, and she checks them off as she packs.

No two families plan exactly the same way. Some prefer to do as much of the cooking at home as possible. Others prefer to stock staples and shop along the way.

Packing your icebox. You can double up on space in your ice chest, refrigerator, or ice box by freezing food, water, and beverages for use as refrigerants. When they thaw, they're ready to use.

A styrene foam ice chest that isn't opened too often will keep meats frozen about 3 days, depending on the weather. To keep meats frozen on extended trips, pack only meats in the chest and use dry ice as an added refrigerant. You can freeze fresh meats such as a large roast (to cook in the Dutch oven when thawed), or hamburger patties stacked in a plastic juice container. Freeze chicken legs and thighs in plastic bags or containers and use them as needed; they thaw quickly when removed from the chest. Steaks and chops can be frozen individually and taken out as needed for each meal.

Other packing tips. Wash vegetables and salad greens at home. The greens can be washed, dried, torn into bite-sized pieces, and stored in plastic bags. They make a good filler in the icebox.

Store silverware and small utensils in a large can. Cut a cardboard box (opened at one end) to fit inside making three compartments. You can carry the can to the table.

For a clean table anywhere, carry three yards of oilcloth rolled on a broom handle—always ready to spread on public picnic tables.

dishes. Use it as fruit for breakfast, a spread for pancakes or French toast, a sauce for gingerbread, or in a cobbler with biscuit mix topping.

Raisins, dates, dried figs, and prunes can be eaten as is or chopped and added to puddings and cereals. Seedless or pitted fruit is easier to use.

Canned fruit. Although it is heavy and space-consuming, canned fruit makes a welcome change from dried fruits. Many varieties are available in 8-ounce cans that serve two.

Canned fruit juice. Canned fruit juices, though not as healthful as frozen or fresh juices, provide a refreshing source of sugar and some vitamin enrichment. A wide variety is available. Small cans of juice are handy for lunch packs if drinking water is not readily available.

Powdered fruit juice. Dehydrated fruit juices offer the most compact method of carrying fruit juice on the camping trip. You can choose from three kinds: powdered synthetic flavors, powdered whole juice, and crystallized whole juice. Whole fruit powders and crystals are available at camp supply stores.

You can carry individual envelopes of dehydrated juice on the trail; mix with water for a refreshing drink.

Eggs

Few camp breakfasts are considered complete without some version of eggs. But they are also needed for some dinner dishes.

Fresh eggs. These should be kept in a cooler, or with ice if possible, if they are to survive the usual two-week vacation. If you are *sure* they are fresh, you may be able to count on them for two weeks without refrigeration if the weather is cool and you can store them in a cool place. Otherwise they will probably not last more than a few days.

Pack eggs carefully for transport. If carried in the store carton, pack on top of groceries and pad with towels. Enclose each carton in a bag to confine any possible leakage.

Fried eggs are a natural at camp, but you can fix them almost any way you do at home. Partially fill the skillet with water and poach them, spooning hot water over their tops as they cook. Or hard-cook some for lunch on the trail.

SOUP STARTERS

The standard first course for dinner is soup. If you are using dried soups, make two packages for four to six people, but reduce the amount of water. Many dried soups combine well. You'll find cream of leek and chicken very good with herbs. Dill weed adds a nice touch to any of the vegetable soups. Curry and ginger root make a spicy tomato soup. Try dried parsley and minced onion in smoky pea. Minestrone and onion soup both benefit from grated Parmesan cheese.

Experiment with combinations you'd never think of at home. Add more vegetables (from packets of peas, beans, tomato, or vegetable flakes), thicken with potato flakes or precooked rice, throw in dehydrated meat balls.

Curried Green Pea Soup

In a pot melt 1 tablespoon margarine with 1 teaspoon curry powder. Add 1 can (11¼ oz.) condensed green pea soup; gradually stir in 1 soup can water and 1 teaspoon instant minced onion. Heat through and serve in cups, topped with crisp, crumbled, cooked bacon, if you wish. Makes 3 to 4 servings.

Sherry Tomato Soup

In a pot combine 1 can (10¾ oz.) condensed tomato soup, ½ soup can water, ¼ teaspoon basil, and 3 tablespoons Sherry. Heat thoroughly. Serve in cups; sprinkle with shredded Parmesan cheese. Makes 3 to 4 servings.

Vegetable Broth

In a pot combine 1 can (24 oz.) cocktail vegetable juice with 2 or 3 teaspoons beef stock base; heat thoroughly. Serve in cups; top with freeze-dried chives. Makes 3 to 4 servings.

Can Opener Minestrone

In a pot slowly heat together 2 cans (10½ oz. each) condensed bean soup, 1 can (1 lb.) stewed tomatoes, and 1 can (about 1 lb.) mixed vegetables, stirring occasionally. If desired, thin soup with water. Top bowls of soup with grated Parmesan cheese. Makes 4 servings.

Or you can scramble eggs with your favorite herbs, instant minced onions, grated Parmesan or Cheddar cheese, diced ham, canned mushrooms, parsley or garlic flakes, or crumbled bacon.

Dehydrated and freeze-dried eggs. These are an excellent substitute for fresh eggs in pancake batter, casseroles, baked dishes, or wherever eggs are cooked with other ingredients. Packaged omelettes (ham, bacon, cheese, Spanish, and Western) are found at camping stores and some food stores. Scrambled eggs, plain or with bacon or ham flavoring, are also available. Try out different brands before you go.

Bacon

Along with eggs, bacon is a camp breakfast staple. It also supplies the fat needed for frying fish, pancakes, potatoes, and other dishes. The types that hold up best in camp are the dry, salty, or well-smoked varieties with a minimum of fat. Ordinary package bacon deteriorates rapidly in camp unless it is refrigerated.

Sliced bacon. The leanest types of packaged bacon are Canadian bacon (also called back bacon) and beef bacon.

Slab bacon. A piece of slab bacon—pork side meat—is a good buy. The rind is good for greasing pans. Slab bacon must be refrigerated.

Canned bacon. Precooked bacon, available in 14-ounce cans, can be kept indefinitely until the can is opened. It should then be handled like regular packaged bacon. Both pork and beef bacon are obtainable in cans from camp supply houses.

Bacon bars. Pre-fried bacon pressed into bars. Use in or with breakfast eggs, crumble into soups, stews, and other dinner dishes. It is ideal for hikers to carry in their lunches.

Note. Bacon shares with ham the honor of being the No. 1 Bear Attractor in the camp cupboard. It seems to draw bears (and porcupines) from miles around. Store it in a bag suspended between trees, well out of the reach of the tallest bear. It can also be kept in a pressure cooker, sealed tight with the relief valve in place, and no scent of its presence will reach the bear. Wipe off all grease on the outside of the container.

Ham and other smoked meats. Ham, like bacon, spoils rapidly without refrigeration. Canned pressed ham, pre-cooked sausage, and Vienna sausages are especially good with fried and scrambled eggs for breakfast. Buy small cans (one-meal size) to avoid spoilage.

Pancakes, biscuits, and toast

Topped with jam, syrup, or honey, they are an important part of most camp breakfasts. Vary them with cornbread, muffins, or fried potatoes.

Packaged mixes. Prepared biscuit mix is a camp staple. Pancakes, cornbread, and biscuits can be prepared right in the frying pan; you may want to try this at home before you go camping.

Some mixes lose their leavening action if they become damp. Cover with plastic or transfer the contents to plastic containers or bags. (Remember to bring the directions on the boxes, unless you already know the recipes by heart.)

Toast. A good alternate for pancakes is either toast or French toast. Bread can be toasted in the skillet with bacon drippings or over the gasoline burner in a toasting rack.

Syrup, honey, and jam. Packages of instant syrup mix which make one cup each are the easiest to take along. If you plan to carry prepared syrup, transfer it to a plastic bottle or jug.

Jam and honey on pancakes, French toast, biscuits and sandwiches provide quick energy and help satisfy the desire for sweets. Whipped honey in tubs is excellent for camping. You can also find honey in plastic squirt bottles at the grocery store. Both jam and honey are available in tubes at camping stores.

Cereals

An old-fashioned bowl of oatmeal is still regarded by some as the mainstay of the camper's breakfast. Instant and cooked whole grain cereals are satisfying, filling, nutritious, and take up less space than cold cereals. The instant varieties are fast-cooking, especially useful at high altitudes. You can vary cereals with fruit, chopped walnuts, wheat germ, brown sugar, cinnamon, or margarine, and see how fast a potful disappears.

Wheat germ, which is rich in food value, has

ONE-POT DINNERS

Many campers build their evening meal around one filling main dish, with meat and vegetables cooked together in one pot. These meals are usually easy to prepare, tasty, and nourishing, and clean-up is greatly simplified.

Mexican Beef and Beans

Melt 1 tablespoon margarine in a large frying pan over medium-high heat. Add 1 pound lean ground beef and cook until brown and crumbly; drain excess fat. Add 2 tablespoons instant minced onion, 1 can (15 oz.) kidney beans, drained, 1 can (10 oz.) enchilada sauce, ¼ teaspoon salt, and ½ teaspoon chile powder. Cover, move pan to lower heat, and let simmer for 10 minutes. Just before serving, stir in 1 cup diced sharp Cheddar cheese. Serve in bowls, topping each with ¼ cup crushed corn chips. Makes 4 servings.

Sloppy Joe Stack

Sauté 1 pound ground beef and 1 large onion, coarsely chopped, in a large kettle, stirring occasionally, until meat is well browned; sprinkle 1 package (1½ oz.) seasoning mix for Sloppy Joe over meat. Add 1 can (6 oz.) tomato paste and 1½ cups water; blend, and cook until mixture thickens, about 5 minutes. Add 1 can (4½ oz.) chopped ripe olives and simmer 10 minutes. Make a pancake batter by combining 1 large box (about 14 oz.) corn muffin mix, 1 egg, and 1¼ cups water and mix until smooth. The batter thickens on standing, and you may need to add more water so batter will be thin. Bake 6 pancakes on a hot, greased griddle, making each pancake 8 inches in diameter. Use 2 pancakes for each stack, spooning some of the meat mixture between the pancakes and over the top. Cut each stack in halves or fourths to serve. Makes 6 to 12 servings.

Tenaya Beans

Cut 1 can (12 oz.) luncheon meat in 1-inch cubes; brown in a large pan in 1 tablespoon margarine until slightly crisp. Drain 1 can (about 9 oz.) sliced pineapple and cut into small pieces right in the can; add to meat along with 1 can (1 lb. 12 oz.) baked beans, 2 tablespoons brown sugar, and ¼ teaspoon ground cloves. Heat slowly, stirring occasionally. Makes 8 servings.

Slices of canned brown bread, wrapped in foil and heated over the coals, make a good accompaniment.

Quick Paella

In a medium-sized pan, stir together 1 package (about 7 oz.) precooked rice, 4 tablespoons instant minced onion, 1 can (1 lb.) stewed tomatoes, 1 can (7½ oz.) minced clams and juices, 1 can (7 or 8 oz.) small oysters and juices, and 1 can (4½ oz.) shrimp, rinsed and drained. Bring to a boil, cover, and simmer for 5 minutes. Remove from heat and let stand tightly covered for 10 more minutes, or until rice is done. Makes 4 or 5 servings.

Smoked Sausage and Beans

Cut 1 package (12 oz.) precooked smoked sausages into bite-sized pieces; brown slowly in a large pan. Drain liquid from 1 can (1 lb.) kidney beans and 1 can (12 oz.) whole kernel corn, and add beans and corn to pan. Add 1 can (8 oz.) tomato sauce and ¼ teaspoon oregano; heat through. Makes 8 servings.

Mexican Fiesta

Empty 1 can (about 15 oz.) tamales into a large greased frying pan; remove outer casings. Cover tamales with 1 can (about 1 lb.) chile with beans and 1 can (about 7 oz.) whole kernel corn, drained. Cover pan and heat slowly (do not mix). Makes 4 servings.

To complete a Mexican-style dinner, prepare a salad of avocado halves with French dressing and serve with heated canned or packaged tortillas.

Tuna with New Potatoes

In a large frying pan brown 3 slices bacon, cut in small pieces; add 1 small onion, finely chopped, and cook until translucent. Drain and dice 1 can (1 lb.) new potatoes and add to frying pan; drain and add 1 can (about 6½ oz.) tuna and add to mixture; heat through. Pass grated Parmesan cheese to sprinkle over the top. Makes 2 or 3 servings.

German-Style Beef

You might serve this with potato pancakes (made from a mix or your own recipe) or over hot cooked egg noodles.

Combine in saucepan 1 can (10¾ oz.) beef gravy, 1 can (12 oz.) roast beef, and ⅓ cup canned prepared mincemeat. Heat mixture, stirring, until simmering. Makes 4 servings.

many other uses in camp. It can be added to pancake, muffin, and certain bread mixes, and used judiciously in stews and other dinner dishes.

Cold cereal, though bulky to pack, is a welcome breakfast variation. For a trail breakfast, many hikers prefer dry cereal fortified with sugar.

Instant breakfast

Although advertised as a complete meal, instant breakfast is a highly nourishing supplement, rather than a meal substitute. It makes a good pick-me-up between meals, especially for children.

LUNCH SUGGESTIONS

Lunches in camp have more latitude than those eaten along the trail. Hikers will want lightweight, high-energy foods.

Bread and crackers

Store the bread in a tightly-closed plastic container to keep it fresh as long as possible.

Here are some tasty alternatives you can buy: compact pumpernickel, rye rounds, canned date and nut bread, zwieback, rye wafers, shredded wheat crackers (they carry better than most crackers), and breadsticks. Most crackers seem to get soggy, too dry, or crumbly.

In some rural areas you may find a locally baked bread specially prepared for prospectors, cowboys, or sheepherders who must cook far from supplies for several days at a stretch.

Sandwich fillings and spreads

Nourishing high protein fillings will be the most satisfying. Buy small-size jars and cans so fillings can be protected as long as possible from exposure to the air. For instance, if you will need about a quart of mayonnaise, buy two pint jars instead of one large jar. The second jar will be in good condition when you open it.

Most plastic-wrapped lunch meats will not keep without refrigeration, and you will probably not want to carry too many cans. Nonetheless, your selection is wide: peanut butter, pasteurized process cheese spreads, hard cheese, dry salami and other sausage slices, tuna, corned beef, chipped beef, deviled ham, and chicken spread.

Both catsup and mustard come in tubes (available in camp supply stores.)

Sweets

Aside from fresh, canned, and dried fruit, the sweets selected for lunch and in-between snacks should be of the non-melt, non-crumbly variety. Hard candies, peanut brittle, and non-melt semisweet chocolate bars make good trail fare; caramels and lemon drops are other favorites.

Fruit crackers and hard or chewy cookies will keep well in plastic bags or containers. Camp supply stores have an amazing variety of lightweight, long-lasting sweets.

Snacks

Snacks are important for the lunch sack, and you have a wide range to choose from. For hikers, these are good: nuts, beef jerky, bacon bars, salami sticks.

In camp these can be varied with celery sticks, (filled with cheese spreads if you prefer), radishes, pickles, olives, and green pepper slices.

Cheese

Select a hard cheese that won't need refrigeration, preferably one wrapped in a wax-impregnated cloth. Recommended are smoked hickory, hard jack, Cheddar, Swiss, Edam, or Gouda; and canned Camembert for the end of your stay. Small jars of pasteurized process cheeses are also practical.

DINNER SUGGESTIONS

Dinner is usually the main meal of the day. Modern camping foods offer an amazing variety.

Soups

A wide choice of delicious dehydrated soups are now available in grocery stores.

You can add variety and body to prepared soups with herbs, vegetable flakes, and chopped meat, vegetables, potatoes, and onions. Combination meat and vegetable soup powders are excellent for enriching the flavor of stews and casseroles. Onion and mushroom soups are particularly versatile in gravies, sauces, with cooked vegetables,

ESPECIALLY FOR BACKPACKERS—DINNER ON THE TRAIL

These recipes rely heavily on freeze-dried foods and prepared sauce and seasoning mixes. Much of the preliminary measuring and preparation can be done at home to keep weight and bulk to a minimum.

Beef Stroganoff with Green Noodles

At home, combine in large bag 2 cans (2 oz. each) freeze-dried beef steaks, 1 envelope (1½ oz.) dry beef stroganoff sauce mix, a small plastic bag containing 1 envelope (about 1½ oz.) dry sour cream sauce mix combined with 3 tablespoons dry skim milk, and a bag of about 6 oz. green noodles. Seal package with these cooking instructions:

Add ½ cup water to sour cream sauce bag and squeeze to mix; set aside at least 10 minutes. Meanwhile bring water to boil (unsalted) for the noodles, and refresh beef steaks in water according to directions on can. Drain and dry beef and brown in 2 tablespoons margarine, add stroganoff sauce mix and about ½ cup water, blending smoothly. Simmer uncovered about 5 minutes, then stir in sour cream sauce and a bit more water if needed. Cook noodles until tender to bite, drain, and serve meat and sauce over them. Makes 4 servings.

Chile Beans and Pork Chops

At home, combine in 1 large package 3 cans (2 oz. each) freeze-dried boneless pork chops, 1 envelope (about 1 oz.) dry brown gravy mix, 1 package (10 oz.) precooked dried chile-flavored beans, and a small bag with 2 tablespoons brown sugar. Seal package with these instructions:

Refresh pork chops in water according to directions on can, drain, dry, then brown in 2 tablespoons margarine. Stir in gravy mix and water as directed on envelope and heat to simmering, stirring. Set aside.

Combine beans with water as directed on package, add brown sugar, and simmer 20 to 30 minutes or until beans are tender to bite. Then stir in pork chops and gravy and heat through. Makes 4 to 5 servings.

Potatoes and Tuna Au Gratin

At home, put the potatoes from 1 package (5½ oz.) au gratin potato mix in a large, heavy plastic bag and add 1 package (1 oz.) dehydrated green beans and ½ teaspoon salt. Open the packet containing cheese sauce mix, dump into a small plastic bag, and seal shut. Put cheese mix, and 1 can (6½ oz.) solid-pack tuna in oil, into the bag with the potatoes. Seal package with these instructions:

Put tomatoes, beans, and salt into a pan and add 3 cups cold water. Cover and bring to boil, then simmer until tender. Drain, leaving about ½ cup liquid in pan. Sprinkle cheese sauce mix over potatoes. Open tuna, break apart, and pour entire contents of can into potatoes. Mix well. If you want a little more sauce, add a few tablespoons of water and heat, stirring. Makes 3 to 4 servings.

Spaghetti with Meatballs in Sauce

At home, in heavy plastic bag combine 1 envelope (1½ oz.) dry spaghetti sauce mix, 1 package (1 oz.) tomato flakes, about 1 tablespoon freeze-dried parsley, 3 or 4 whole black peppers, about 1 tablespoon instant minced onion, a generous pinch mixed herbs seasoning, and 2 cans (1¾ oz.) freeze-dried meatballs. In separate bags, put 8 oz. spaghetti and about ½ cup grated Parmesan cheese, then place in sauce bag. Seal package with these cooking instructions:

Pour sauce mix including meatballs into pan, add 1 small clove garlic, 2 tablespoons margarine, and 3 cups water; blend and bring to boiling. Simmer 20 to 30 minutes, stirring frequently as mixture tends to stick.

Also bring to boil a large quantity of water. When sauce is about ready, cook spaghetti in water until tender to bite—takes 5 to 10 minutes. Drain spaghetti and blend with sauce. Sprinkle with cheese. Makes 3 to 4 servings.

Mountain Beans

At home, combine in a large plastic bag 1 package (10 oz.) dehydrated cooked seasoned beans, 1 package (1⅝ oz.) chile sauce mix, 2 teaspoons chile powder, ¼ cup instant toasted onions, and 1 package (1 oz.) dehydrated tomato flakes. Pour 1 package (4 oz.) dehydrated cooked ground beef into a small plastic bag and seal; place in larger bag with beans. Seal package with these cooking instructions:

Pour all but ground beef into pan. Add 5½ cups water and let stand 10 minutes. Cover, bring to a boil, and simmer 10 minutes. Add ground beef and continue cooking, covered, until beans are tender to bite; stir frequently. Add more water if needed. Makes 4 to 5 servings.

COOKING ON THE TRAIL

What equipment is necessary for cooking on the trail? Here is one expert backpacker's list:

One cup per person, aluminum with stainless steel rim and handle to protect lips and fingers.

One stainless steel soup spoon per person. Carry one extra for cooking and serving.

Nest of cooking pots. Lightest weight available; take along only the 6-cup coffee pot, the 1 and 2-quart pots, and frying pan which doubles as lid.

One tomato can (16 or 17 oz. size). Attach a thin wire handle; this fits inside the coffee pot.

One pot lifter.

One sharp knife, medium sized, in a sheath. It should be strong enough and large enough to cut small pieces of wood as well as food.

One small spatula.

One small grill, rectangular shaped, 4 to 6 inches long, to make cooking fireplace.

One-burner Alpine stove, for rainy areas or where wood is scarce (optional).

Two steel wool soap pads, for scrubbing dishes. Put each in separate plastic bag.

Paper towels, with cardboard roll removed.

Heavy duty aluminum foil (1-2 square feet) for keeping food hot. Wash and use again.

Folding plastic bucket, for toting water or for personal washing (optional).

Lightweight plastic bag (such as one from cleaners) for covering charred cooking equipment.

Five heavy plastic bags (2 gallon size) for packing food.

One-quart heavy plastic bag for carrying water and mixing juice for breakfast and lunch.

Pipe cleaners, rubber bands, or garden twist-ems for tying bags.

This is a very modest kitchen. All meals are eaten from a cup with a spoon, and cooking pots double as mixing bowls. The spatula can also serve to drain liquids from foods. The foil can make an extra lid for small pots or an extra pan or plate.

Packing food. Repack the food in small, meal-size amounts wherever possible. Use strong plastic bags (be sure to label them and include cooking instructions) for more flexibility and less weight. Remove freeze-dried food packets from boxes and puncture each packet with a pin *near the top of the envelope* so they will lie flat. Do not puncture in the middle; you will use the packet for soaking, then drain to cook.

The five heavy plastic bags are used as follows: breakfasts and dinners in one each; lunch in two (foods are bulkier); basic foods in the fifth bag (coffee, tea, salt, pepper, sugar, margarine, powdered milk, cocoa, and seasonings).

---

and in egg and meat dishes. Chicken and beef stock, as well as bouillon, make good starters for homemade soup.

Meats

If you are camping without refrigeration and without access to fresh meat, you will need to rely on canned, packaged, or freeze-dried meats.

Fresh and frozen meat. Frozen meat or chicken can be taken to camp for the first dinner, but without refrigeration meat spoils quickly. A large frozen steak or roast may take several days to thaw, particularly if it is kept on ice in a cooler and wrapped in foil and newspaper.

Smoked and dried meats. Precooked hams are a poor choice because they do not keep. Dry, hard,

sugar-cured hickory-smoked ham sealed in a cloth sack will keep longest. Cover ham with a vinegar-soaked cloth to help preserve it.

Salt pork is a useful item. You can grease the skillet with it, fry it in place of bacon, or add it to bean dishes and chowders. A pound is ample.

Freeze-dried meats and dinners. The most revolutionary aid to camp cooking in recent years is freeze-dried meats and meals. When rehydrated and cooked, freeze-dried foods are in general much closer to fresh flavors than those of ordinary dehydrated foods.

You'll find a lengthy list to choose from, and new ones are being developed all the time. You can find meats only (pork chops, meat balls, hamburger, shrimp); one-dish meals (beef and chicken stews, chile with beans, shrimp creole); and even complete meals (pork chop with applesauce and potatoes, Swiss steak with peas and potatoes).

Freeze-dried foods are considerably more expensive than fresh, canned, or packaged foods. However, some campers feel that the extra expense is justified by the quality and convenience.

You may want to try some at home. You may also find the estimates of servings over-optimistic.

Some freeze-dried foods are available in supermarkets; most camp supply stores carry a full line.

Canned meats. The choice in canned meats is a broad one—ham, hamburgers, meat balls, beef and pork patties, boned pork chops, beef steaks, chicken, frankfurters, corned beef, tuna, and luncheon meat. Some can be served either hot or cold. While bulky to carry, canned meats are a camp standby when fresh meat runs out.

Many other meat dinners come in cans—hash, stew, spaghetti and meat balls, tamales, enchiladas, ravioli, lasagna, chile, etc.

Packaged dinners. You can find a cosmopolitan variety of packaged dinners at any supermarket. They are quick and simple to prepare, light and easy to pack, and relatively inexpensive.

You can supplement or extend them for a hearty meal by adding canned or dried meats, beans, cheese, tomatoes, vegetables, sauces, or soups.

Gravies and sauces

Almost every kind of gravy or sauce invented has been converted to packaged instant mix. You can improve on many canned meats and prepared dishes by adding a tasty gravy or sauce.

Sauces and seasoning mixes are especially useful at camp: You can find tomato-based sauces, including spaghetti sauce mix, for pasta, chile, rice; scallopini, stroganoff, and à la king sauce mixes; instant sour cream mix.

Canned creamy sauces—cheese, white, hollandaise, and Welsh rarebit—are delicious with canned fish and vegetables, and no one has found a really good substitute for canned tomato sauce or tomato paste.

Potatoes

Fresh potatoes take up a lot of room, but they last through the entire vacation. Some cooks find too many uses for them to leave them at home; others depend mainly on dehydrated or canned potatoes.

MORE DINNERS FOR THE TRAIL

Here are three more dinner ideas using lightweight convenience foods.

Rice and Peas with Ham

At home, combine in a large, heavy plastic bag the rice from 1 package (5 oz.) rice casserole with cheese and sauce mix, and 1 package (2½ oz.) dehydrated green peas. Empty sauce mix into small plastic bag; seal. Empty 2 cans (1 oz. each) freeze-dried ham into a medium-sized plastic bag and seal. Put sauce and ham in with the rice. Seal package with these cooking instructions:

Pour rice mixture into pan and add 2¾ cups cold water; stir to moisten, and let stand 15 minutes. In the meantime, add enough water to ham in plastic bag to cover meat; let stand 10 minutes.

Cover pan and bring to a boil. Simmer, stirring frequently; add more liquid if needed to prevent sticking. Drain ham and add to cooked rice; sprinkle rice with cheese mixture, blend well, and serve. Makes 3 to 4 servings.

Chicken Stew and Dumplings

At home, into a plastic bag put 2 packages (6½ oz. each) dehydrated chicken stew. In smaller bag measure 2 cups biscuit mix. Seal package with these cooking instructions:

Prepare chicken stew according to package directions, adding 1 additional cup water for each package. To make dumplings, dilute ½ cup evaporated milk with ½ cup water, pour into biscuit mix, and stir until combined. When stew is done, drop small mounds of dough on top of simmering liquid. Cook uncovered for 10 minutes; cover, cook 10 more minutes. Makes 6 servings.

Trail Paella

At home, into a large, heavy plastic bag empty 2 cans (1 oz. each) freeze-dried shrimp, 1 package (4 oz.) dehydrated cooked ground chicken, 2 teaspoons onion powder, ¼ teaspoon oregano, 1 package (6 oz.) Spanish-style seasoned rice (open packet of seasonings and mix with rice), and 1 package (2½ oz.) dehydrated green peas. Seal package with these cooking instructions:

Pour contents of bag into pan, and add 4½ cups cold water; mix and let stand 10 minutes. Bring to a boil, covered, and simmer until rice is tender and liquid absorbed; stir frequently. Makes 4 servings.

Diced, dehydrated potatoes. A 5-ounce package equals two pounds of fresh potatoes. They can be used for hash-browns or mashed potatoes.

Instant mashed potatoes. At high altitude it's a good idea to cook them in the water and milk over the fire for a minute—stirring all the time—instead of mixing in the hot liquid off the fire. You should add more liquid than usual (about ½ cup more for four persons), as liquid evaporates faster the higher the altitude.

Instant potato powder can also be used to thicken and flavor gravies and sauces. Stir in only a little at a time until the gravy is the consistency you want.

Canned potatoes. If you have space for them, canned potatoes are handy when you don't want to take time or are too tired to cook fresh ones.

Rice

Both instant and quick-cooking rice need special cooking in high altitudes.

When you cook *instant* rice at altitudes over 3,000 feet, boil it 1 or 2 minutes before you remove the covered kettle from the fire or steam. The *quick-cooking* type should cook 11 to 12 minutes instead of the usual 9.

Rice can be flavored in many ways—by cooking with beef or chicken bouillon, or by adding any of the following: dehydrated soup mixes, tomato juice or diluted tomato sauce or paste, processed cheese spreads, packaged sauce mixes.

For dessert, add raisins or other dried fruits stewed soft to the cooked rice. Combine this with ½ cup each milk and sugar, a couple of eggs, flavoring, and appropriate spices, and bake.

FOIL COOKERY

You can bake, broil, and eat on aluminum foil, saving pots, pans, plates, and energy. Here are some things you can try:

• Bake potatoes, apples, or corn tightly wrapped in foil.

• Cook a stew sealed in foil.

• Make foil cups and cook muffins or biscuits.

To save on dishwashing, you can lay foil inside a skillet and throw away the lining after the food is cooked. Or cover the outside of pans being used over a wood fire to keep them from being blackened by soot.

Food cooked in sealed foil won't brown much, nor will it get a smoky flavor from the campfire.

Kitchen tongs or heavy gloves are needed for picking foil-cooked foods off the coals. Often you can serve the food right in its foil container.

The right kind of coals is the most important factor when cooking in foil; a blazing fire just won't do. Until you become expert on heat and timing for foil cooking, you may want to peek inside the wrapping occasionally to check the cooking progress.

Use heavy duty foil and fold it double. Or you can buy foil pans in grocery stores; the ridged-bottom type is excellent for cooking bacon.

To cook lyonnaise potatoes. Cut a large potato and an onion into thin slices, mix, add a little salt and a bit of butter, wrap in foil, and cook for 15 minutes on the coals.

To broil a steak. Arrange the steak on top of a sheet of foil, but do not wrap. Place directly on top of the hot coals and broil, turning once. The length of time required for broiling depends on how well cooked you like your steak.

To make meatball stew. Shape lean ground beef into small balls; cook with canned potatoes and onions (drained) and frozen mixed vegetables *or* sliced raw potatoes and carrot chunks. Sprinkle with salt and pepper. Spoon over about 3 tablespoons canned condensed tomato, Cheddar cheese, or mushroom soup, catsup, or tomato sauce. Fold foil securely in center and at ends. Place on hot coals for about 20 to 30 minutes.

To bake potatoes. Wash potatoes and wrap individually in several thicknesses of foil. Rake back coals, drop in wrapped potatoes, and cover with coals. Bake for 1½ to 2 hours, depending on size of potatoes. Use a splinter of wood to test for doneness before removing from the coals.

To bake apples. Cut a slice from the top, remove the core, sprinkle a tablespoon of brown sugar and a few raisins or miniature marshmallows in the hollow. Place on a square of foil and bring corners up around the apple, twisting them together at the top to secure. Bake 30 minutes.

Vegetables

The car camper can combine fresh, canned, and dehydrated vegetables, depending on the amount of weight he wishes to pack and the length of time he will be away from stores.

Fresh vegetables. Leafy and head vegetables wilt and dry out rapidly after the first few days. Tomatoes (buy slightly underripe), green peppers, celery, cucumbers, radishes, and green beans usually last a little longer. Banana and acorn squash are fairly good survivors, but bulky. Onions and root vegetables—potatoes, yams, beets, turnips, and carrots—will keep the longest. Fresh corn on the cob, though not long-lasting, tastes particularly good when foil wrapped and baked in coals.

Canned vegetables. Space limitations and your personal preferences will determine the kinds and amounts you take to camp. Canned tomatoes, green beans, peas, and corn can be heated and served, or they can be added to one-dish meals. Corn niblets can be mixed with pancake batter and fried as corn fritters, to be served with jam or syrup. Creamed corn mixed with powdered eggs and flour or crumbs makes a good corn pudding.

Hominy grits are handy both for cereal and frying. Fried hominy with plenty of brown sugar is a substantial addition to breakfast.

Dehydrated vegetables. These vegetables take up much less space and weight than either canned or fresh, but they are more expensive, less tasty, and some require prolonged soaking.

Dehydrated potatoes, carrots, beets, and cabbage are regarded as the most palatable; all must be soaked at least an hour and cooked well. Instant chopped onions improve many egg, vegetable, or meat dishes.

Beans

Dried beans must be soaked overnight. Cook with seasonings in a pressure cooker to minimize work and cooking time. Pre-cooked beans are also available.

Canned baked beans can be perked up with bacon, onions, dry mustard, Worcestershire, or salt pork. Canned kidney beans and chile beans are also staples.

SIDE DISHES AND SALADS

Here are several dishes and salads to accompany the main part of the meal.

Onion Pilaff

Melt 2 tablespoons margarine in a heavy saucepan; stir in 1½ cups bulgur or quick-cooking cracked wheat and brown for 2 or 3 minutes. Add 1 package (amount for 3 or 4 servings) dried onion soup mix and 3 cups water. Cover, bring to a boil, then simmer for about 15 minutes. Makes 6 servings.

Zesty Fried Potatoes

Melt 4 tablespoons margarine or bacon drippings in a large frying pan; fry 1 package (9 oz.) hashed brown potatoes as instructed on the package (or 3 potatoes, peeled, cooked, and diced) until done. Just before removing from the fire, sprinkle 3 tablespoons vinegar over the top; mix with a fork. Season with salt and pepper. Makes 3 servings.

Mexican Zucchini

Parboil small zucchinis for 3 minutes (either at home or at the campsite) and cool. For each zucchini, cut a long, narrow strip (about ¼-inch wide) of canned green chile; and slightly larger strips of jack cheese (about 5 inches long and ½-inch wide). Slit zucchinis from end to end, leaving underside attached. Place a strip of chile and a strip of cheese in each zucchini; wrap each with a strip of uncooked bacon, securing both ends of bacon with toothpicks. Place on barbecue or in a hinged broiler and cook over medium heat, turning, for 15 to 20 minutes or until bacon is crisp and zucchini tender. Plan on 1 or 2 small zucchinis per person.

Apple Salad

Halve and core 4 large red apples (do not peel). Cut apples, 2 peeled oranges, and 2 stalks celery into small pieces. Mix with ¼ cup mayonnaise. Sprinkle chopped nuts on top. Makes 6 servings.

Cucumber Salad

Peel and dice 2 cucumbers. Cut 2 cups seedless grapes in half. Dress with ¼ cup creamy French dressing. Makes 6 servings.

Desserts

Camp desserts are easy to shop for. A few cans of fruit, some packages of instant pudding and dehydrated fruits, and a few boxes of cake mix, and you can cap every dinner with a suitable dessert.

Puddings. Canned puddings, ready to eat, are available in a variety of flavors and serving sizes. Instant puddings, which you mix with cold milk, are preferred to those which must be cooked. Vary them by adding chopped dried fruits, crushed candy brittle, chocolate bits, nut meats, or crumbled cookies.

Prepared cake mixes. A camp stove or reflector oven bakes cakes satisfactorily if you turn the pan as necessary to keep the edges from burning while the cake is baking. One side of these ovens is often a little hotter than the other. If the top seems to be getting too brown, place a piece of foil over the cake to reflect away part of the heat.

Many prepared mixes have high altitude instructions printed on the box.

Probably the most satisfactory type of camp cake is the upside-down fruit variety, which you can bake right in your frying pan.

Prepared frostings. Both packaged and canned frostings are quick to mix and easy to spread. Use them as pudding sauce or to make quick candy.

Prepared pie shells. Fill with prepared pudding or pie mix, or with canned fruit pie filling.

CONDIMENTS

A few small items will perk up anything that comes out of a can or a box.

Bouillon cubes

Beef or chicken bouillon cubes do double duty as flavoring for soups, gravies, and stews, and as a nourishing hot drink.

Salt

Camp diet should provide plenty of salt, especially if the weather is hot and campers will be exercising strenuously. Use a moisture-proof container.

Herbs, spices, seasonings

Although not really necessary, certain herbs and spices will add zest to your dishes. Bring the ones you use most often at home.

You'll probably want black pepper; others to consider are chili powder, paprika, oregano, dried parsley. Cloves, cinnamon, and nutmeg are good with fruits. Worcestershire perks up many dishes. Mustard and catsup are both available in tubes at camp supply stores. You may also want to include garlic salt, instant minced onions, vegetable flakes, barbecue seasoning, or any others on which you rely.

All herbs and spices should be in moisture-proof containers; pharmacy pill bottles are handy for small amounts. You might want to make a cloth roll-up kit to hold your small spice containers.

Butter vs. margarine

Butter has its limitations in camp. It requires refrigeration, or at least a cooler, or it will spoil rapidly. Vacuum-packed cans of butter keep indefinitely until opened, then it turns rancid as rapidly as regular store butter.

Margarine is the camper's standby. It does not need refrigeration and will survive two weeks or more if kept in a cool place. Some campers transfer it to screw-top jars for cleanliness and safekeeping.

Like all fats, butter and margarine are attractive to roaming animals and should be stored out of the reach of four-footed thieves.

BEVERAGES

Beverages made from powder mixed with water or dry skim milk—instant coffee, tea, or cocoa—are the lightest to carry and easiest to prepare.

Coffee

The rich aroma of coffee simmering over a wood fire is one memorable sensation of camping. Some campers insist on camp coffee, brewed in a pot to a hearty consistency. Other campers prefer the convenience of the instant varieties, made in the cup and eliminating the pot.

Ground coffee comes in cans of several sizes. You can buy instant coffee in jars of various sizes,

DESSERTS TO COMPLETE DINNER
WITH A FLOURISH

Usually camp desserts are fairly simple—often instant pudding or fruit—but sometimes you want a special dessert.

Mountain Orange Dessert

Make 1 package (about 3¾ oz.) instant vanilla pudding as directed on the package, using 1 cup evaporated milk diluted with 1 cup water as a substitute for the milk. Drain 1 can (11 oz.) mandarin oranges and stir in. Keep in a cool place until time to serve. Makes 4 servings.

Skillet Cherry Pudding

In a large frying pan melt ¼ cup margarine; brown 2 slices white bread, cubed, in the margarine. Sprinkle in ¼ cup sugar and stir until it dissolves. Stir in 1 can (1 lb. 5 oz.) cherry pie filling; heat through. Sprinkle with 2 tablespoons sliced almonds and serve. Makes 6 servings.

Baked Apples and Cheese

Open cans of baked apples (packed 2 or 3 to a can in heavy syrup), cover can with foil, and place on grill for 20 minutes, or until hot. Spoon out one apple for each serving, top with the syrup. Serve with Cheddar cheese.

Campers' Fruit Pie

Mix together 1½ cups prepared biscuit mix, 2 tablespoons sugar, and 4 tablespoons dry skim milk; add 1 cup water and stir until well blended and free of lumps. (If mixture thickens on standing, stir in a little more water to make a thin batter.) Bake eight 6-inch pancakes on a hot, greased griddle. Add 1 tablespoon lemon juice to 1 can (1 lb. 5 oz.) prepared fruit pie filling (cherry, apple, or blueberry) in the can, and stir in. Place a large spoonful of pie filling on each pancake and roll up. Sprinkle with sugar before serving. Makes 8 servings.

Hot Apple Sauce with Gingerbread

You can make the gingerbread at home with a mix, wrap tightly in foil, and bring to camp. In camp, remove lid and label from 1 can (1 lb. 4 oz.) apple sauce; cover can with foil and place on grill for about 15 minutes until hot. Spoon hot apple sauce over gingerbread squares.

Chocolate Pudding

Combine 1 package (4 oz.) chocolate-flavored pudding mix with ¾ cup low-fat dry milk product (made with cream) in a pan, and add 1¾ cups cold water. Bring to a boil, stirring; remove from heat and cover. Cool before serving. Makes 3 to 4 servings.

Lemon Tapioca with Prunes

Combine 1 package (3¼ oz.), ¾ cup low-fat dry milk product (made with cream), and 1 cup coarsely chopped pitted prunes in pan. Add 1¾ cups cold water, stir, and let stand 10 minutes. Bring to a rolling boil, stirring. Cover and cool before serving. Makes 3 to 4 servings.

Grilled Cherry Shortcake

Slice a commercial pound cake in ¾-inch slices (1 slice per serving). Brown both sides of each slice in a lightly oiled frying pan on the grill. Remove slices, spread each with a ¼-inch layer of softened cream cheese; spoon canned cherry pie filling over the top.

Instant Cocoa Mix

Make this mix at home for quick preparation in camp. Combine 1 cup unsweetened cocoa, 1 cup sugar, 4 cups dry skim milk, ¼ teaspoon salt. Mix thoroughly and store in a plastic container with a tight-fitting cover. To make hot cocoa, use 1½ cups mix for each quart water.

Mexican Chocolate

Prepare a rich hot chocolate, using larger amounts of chocolate than directions indicate. Add a dash of rum to each cupful; stir with cinnamon stick.

or in individual cup-size envelopes. Freeze-dried instant coffee is also widely available.

Tea

The mountaineer's favorite drink is not coffee, but tea. Tea is less bulky and yields more cups per pound, and tea bags are easily carried in pocket or pack. Instant powdered tea in foil envelopes can be mixed with cold water. Some blends include citrus flavorings and sugar.

Milk

Today's camper has the advantage of a wide choice of milk products and even some non-dairy substitutes.

Fresh milk. No problem if you are camping near a store. You may want to supplement it with canned or dry skim milk in cooking.

Evaporated milk in cans. Since the advent of dry skim milk and cream, evaporated milk at camp is a matter of preference. It is used mostly in cooking, as few people like its strong taste on cereal or diluted for drinking. Small-sized cans are more practical for camp use.

Dried milk. Easy to pack and carry, it does not require refrigeration. It comes in two forms—whole and skim. Dried whole milk is sold in cans, and when mixed with water tastes almost exactly like fresh milk. It does not keep well after opening.

Dried skim milk is packed in air and water-tight foil bags enclosed in cardboard cartons. It is fine for cooking and baking, lighter to carry, and less expensive. Any dried milk tastes better if it is served cold and has been allowed to stand for awhile before it is drunk.

The easiest way to mix it is to shake it with water in specially designed plastic shakers with a pouring hole in the top.

One caution about storing dried milk or any mix containing it: It must be kept in a tightly closed container. If it gets moist it will become lumpy and may develop an odd flavor. Moreover, the fat content may turn rancid.

Powdered cream and non-dairy creamers

These have become a popular replacement for evaporated milk in coffee. A spoonful dissolves instantly in hot liquid (but not in cold). It comes in jars and in individual foil envelopes.

Chocolate drinks

Instant cocoa mixes containing sugar and dry skim milk are the most popular at camp because they merely require adding hot water. (Not all kinds have dry skim milk added; be sure to read the label carefully.) The mix also comes packaged in one-cup envelopes.

A powdered chocolate malt drink can be obtained at camp supply stores.

Flavored powdered drinks

These have been developed as high-energy sources for campers and are found at camp supply stores. They include milk-shake mixes—strawberry, vanilla, chocolate—and vanilla eggnog mix.

Fruit-flavored drinks are extensive—boysenberry, grape, cherry, raspberry, fruit punch; lemon, lime, orange, and pineapple combinations—even tomato juice crystals.

COOKING TROUT

You can poach, steam, or bake trout, but most campers agree that there's no substitute for pan-fried trout—golden brown and crusty outside; flaky, tender, and moist inside. Not being a fatty fish, trout must be cooked with added fat, preferably bacon fat. Bacon drippings carries its own salt and adds a flavor all its own. Other favorites are olive oil, salad oil, and half butter-half oil.

Most fishermen agree on one basic fact: don't overcook. Too much heat—if only for a few minutes—will dry out even the sweetest flavored trout.

To pan-fry small trout, clean them and remove heads, if you wish. Sprinkle lightly with salt and pepper. Roll in cornmeal or a mixture of half cornmeal and half flour to coat all over. Put enough bacon drippings or other fat in the frying pan to coat bottom well. Heat pan until it is hot, but not smoky. Put fish in pan without crowding. Cook quickly until crisp and brown on one side, then turn to brown on other side. Continue cooking just until fish is flaky inside.

CHECKLIST OF CAMPING FOOD

No camper will want to take every item listed below on a camping trip, and some will wish to add items we have omitted. This listing is digested from the fuller discussion of camp foods on the previous pages, and is included to help you prepare your shopping list.

BEVERAGES

Coffee, ground
Coffee, instant
Tea, bags or leaves
Tea, powdered
Cocoa, instant
Chocolate drinks
Milk, fresh
Milk, canned
Milk, powdered whole
Milk, powdered skim
Cream, powdered
Instant breakfast
Fruit juice, canned
Fruit juice, concentrated
Fruit juice, dehydrated
Fruit-flavored drinks, canned
Fruit-flavored drinks, dehydrated
Tomato juice, canned

_____
_____

FRESH FOODS

Bread
Eggs
Meat
Fruit
Vegetables
Potatoes
Onions

_____
_____

CANNED FOODS

Soup
Meat, poultry
Fish, shellfish
Vegetables
Potatoes
Beans
Date and nut bread
Tomato sauce, paste
Cream sauces
Relishes
Fruit

_____
_____

DEHYDRATED AND DRIED FOODS

Soup
*Eggs, scrambled
*Omelettes
*Fruit
*Meat
One-dish meals, freeze-dried
Dinners, freeze-dried
*Vegetables
*Potatoes
Onions
Mushrooms

_____

*Including freeze-dried

STAPLES

Flour
Sugar (white, brown, powdered)
Cornstarch
Salt pork
Oil
Vinegar
Powdered eggs
Macaroni
Noodles
Spaghetti
Rice, quick-cooking
Cereal, hot
Cereal, cold
Wheat germ

_____
_____

FLAVORINGS

Salt
Pepper
Spices
Herbs
Vegetable flakes
Instant chopped onions
Bacon-flavored seasoning
Chicken and beef bouillon cubes
Maple flavoring
Vanilla extract

_____

SNACKS

Dry sausage sticks, slices
Beef jerky
Bacon bars
Hard cheese
Nuts
Hard candy
Non-melt chocolate bars
Marshmallows
Popcorn (kernels)

_____

PACKAGED FOODS AND MIXES

Prepared dinners
Pancake mix
Biscuit mix
Cornbread mix
Muffin mix
Cake mix
Breadsticks
Melba toast
Pretzels
Wafers (rye, wheat)
Zwieback
Gravy and sauce mixes
Seasoning mixes
Salad dressings
Mashed potatoes
Instant puddings
Cake frostings
Hard cookies

_____
_____

SPREADS

Margarine
Catsup
Mustard
Mayonnaise
Peanut butter
Processed cheese spreads
Jam
Syrup
Honey

_____

Making camp

The cardinal rule of experienced campers is: Get to the campsite early. This usually means pulling in to your selected campsite several hours before dinner or, at latest, before sundown.

There are several reasons. With the increased overcrowding of public campgrounds—even on regular summer weekends—you have a much better chance of picking your site, or getting one at all.

Some popular parks are filled to capacity by mid-afternoon, particularly on weekends. If you find the campground filled, you have time to drive on to another camp. If the campground is not heavily used, you can choose the most attractive of several sites. By dark all good spots will be occupied, and late arrivals must take any free site.

Traffic may be lighter if you start early, allowing you a faster trip. If you are driving through hot areas, morning temperatures will be cooler.

And finally, you will have a chance to set up camp in a complete and orderly fashion if you arrive before late afternoon or evening.

CHOOSING A SITE

Here are some things to consider in picking out a campsite:

Improved campgrounds. Often the choice is limited to a few that are unoccupied. If you have a choice of sites, pick one that is not too close to water (chilly at night, may be in the path of fishermen and other campers, likely to have mosquitoes), and that receives morning sun and afternoon shade. If you're hoping for quiet, check out the surrounding sites for babies, children, and dogs.

Unimproved areas. Ground should slope enough to drain off rain water, but not so steeply that the pitch makes sleeping uncomfortable. Soil texture should permit water to be quickly absorbed, but

should not be so sandy that it will not hold tent stakes.

The site should be at least 15 feet above water to avoid morning mist, but close enough for carrying water. Firewood should also be located within a reasonable distance.

The site should be sufficiently exposed and elevated to permit the sun to dry the ground and tents after rain or heavy dew, and to capture moving air currents, both for ventilation and for dispelling insects; hollows attract mosquitoes, mist, and cold air. The site should not be on a crest where strong winds blow, or where lightning might strike a high point.

You should also check for dead or leaning trees that might topple in the wind, and if camping at the base of a cliff, for boulders poised overhead.

In places where flash floods may occur, watch for eroded soil, uprooted trees, branches caught against trees or boulders. If these signs are present, choose a site well above the indicated flood level, and avoid gullies or canyons.

CAMP LAYOUT

In an improved campground, the arrangement of camping equipment is pretty well determined by the layout of the site. If you have a free hand in arranging your camp, block the area into activity zones: sleeping, cooking and dining, cleanup, and loafing. Unload appropriate equipment in each zone.

Sleeping area. Choose a level spot for the tent—under trees in a hot campground, on the edge of a clearing in a cool one. Ideally, back the tent toward the prevailing wind and face it toward morning sun. The door should face the living area.

If necessary, level the ground; remove twigs and rocks, and fill in small depressions. If the ground is damp, lay down a waterproof ground

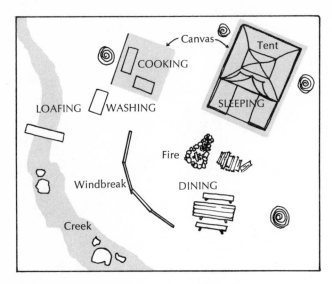

IDEAL CAMP LAYOUT has campsite blocked into activity areas. Camp faces southeast to catch morning sun.

cloth to prolong the life of the tent floor. Protect the floor from punctures by putting plywood or heavy cardboard under any camp furniture which might dig into the soil (or slip crutch tips over furniture feet).

Where summer showers are common, ditch around your tent. Dig a trench about 4 inches wide and 4 inches deep to keep rain water from running into the tent. Fill in with pebbles where the ditch passes the tent door so it won't cave in. Dig a branch trench leading away from the main one to carry water away from the tent.

When a rainstorm appears imminent, slacken ropes and check stakes; canvas shrinks when wet, and sometimes stakes uproot and loops rip off if too tight.

Cooking-dining area. Select an area sheltered from wind so that cooking and dining will not be disrupted by gusts. If no natural protection exists, use a canvas tarp to make a vertical windscreen. In a cool campground, set up your portable equipment in the open; in a hot area, under sheltering branches. If there is any possibility of rain, stretch a canvas fly above the area, and guy it with rope to surrounding trees. The cooking area should be relatively near the water supply.

Loafing area. Provide a cleared but sheltered place for hammock or folding chairs for reading, playing games, mending fishing tackle, or snoozing.

Washroom area. Hang up the wash basin and portable medicine chest, tie a cake of soap to a cord and dangle it from a branch; string a clothesline.

COLLECTING FIREWOOD

In many popular camping areas, firewood has been picked clean by previous campers. You may want to bring wood from home. Some parks have wood for sale at moderate cost.

In most areas you are not permitted to cut standing timber for firewood. You must rely on fallen branches and trees for fuel. Dead branches on standing trees may be used; high branches can sometimes be pulled off with a weighted rope. Hardwoods (from deciduous trees) burn longer than softwoods and provide coals for cooking.

Begin scouting for firewood as soon as your gear is unloaded. Chop, saw, or break wood to usable lengths and stack near the fire. To protect from moisture, cover wood with a tarp or pile under a table. Store some kindling inside the tent as extra insurance. Even when the night is clear, frost or morning dew can dampen wood.

BUILDING A FIRE

As long as you use dry wood and remember to set it loosely in place so air can reach the flames, you should have no difficulty in building a suitable campfire. You need good kindling, and you may want to bring some old candle stubs or commercial fire kindlers; handle fire-starting liquids carefully.

Before building a campfire, clear a 10-foot circle down to bare ground, removing accumulated needles, twigs, and bark. Use rocks or logs to contain your fire and for convenience in cooking.

Start with easily ignited materials—a wad of newspapers and a pyramid of thin wood and shavings. Light with a match, and when the little fire is burning briskly, add larger sticks, gradually building up to sizable pieces of wood as the fire takes hold. When the larger pieces are burning well, add more wood and then leave the fire alone for awhile; let the fire burn down, until it begins to form coals. If coals are insufficient, add more wood and wait awhile longer. *Don't start cooking before the fire is right.* In the meantime, you can complete other preparations for the meal.

Put out the fire with plenty of water. Pay special attention to smoldering ends of larger logs; turn them over and soak thoroughly with water or with several inches of sand.

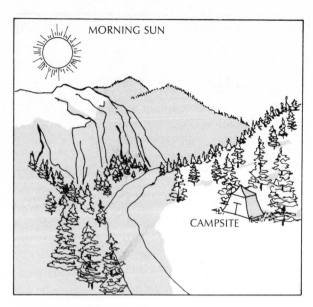

EAST OR SOUTHEAST EXPOSURE at the edge of a clearing gives campsite warmth from the morning sun.

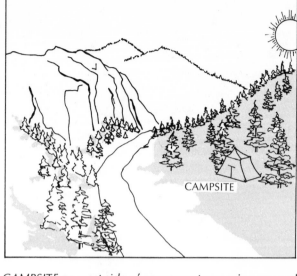

CAMPSITE on west side of canyon gets morning sun and is protected from the oppressive afternoon heat.

Building a fire in wet weather. On a rainy day when the firewood is soaked, starting a campfire can be a difficult and shivery job.

Dry kitchen matches (kept in a waterproof container) are the first necessity. If wood is damp, you'll need a kindler—any substance which will ignite quickly and burn long enough to dry and ignite some of the damp wood around it. Several commercial types are available at sporting goods stores. In addition to using candle stubs, you can make kindlers at home: Roll and tie sections of newspapers in tight rolls 1½ inches across and soak in paraffin. When hard, cut in short sections.

Wet weather fires must be strong enough to generate the necessary heat to dry out the wood as well as to ignite it. The dry kindling you placed in your tent, along with the covered firewood, should get the fire going. Once it is burning briskly, damp wood can be added gradually.

Even in a rainstorm, there are sources of comparatively dry wood. Dead branches and twigs underneath heavily needled conifer limbs will be dry; you can also sometimes find dry wood under fallen trees; and most non-rooted logs and stumps will yield dry wood when they are split.

ORGANIZING CAMP WORK

Nothing spoils a camping vacation more thoroughly than unequal distribution of housekeeping chores. The most painless method is to divide the camp jobs into well-defined tasks and assign full responsibility for each to a specific individual, according to each camper's abilities. Even the least skilled member can draw water, air bedding, wash dishes, or gather wood. You may want the most accomplished cook to prepare all the meals. It usually works best to rotate assignments so no one person gets stuck with a disagreeable chore throughout the stay.

Duty list for making camp

1. Pitch tent
2. Blow up air mattresses, arrange sleeping bags, clothes
3. Gather wood and build cooking fire
4. Draw water
5. Set up cooking, dining, bathroom centers
6. If required, dig latrine and garbage pit
7. Prepare dinner

Day-to-day responsibilities

Every-day jobs in camp:

Camp fireman. Gathers and cuts firewood as needed; protects stacked wood from weather and keeps supply of kindling dry; builds cooking fires and campfires; douses fires when no longer needed; custodian of tools, fire starters, fuel.

DAYTIME WINDS blow off the water and travel up canyons. The water is cooler than the surrounding land.

NIGHT WINDS blow the opposite way. Place a tarpaulin in the path of the wind for nighttime comfort.

Camp cook(s). Can be three persons—one to get breakfast, one to make light camp lunches, and one to cook dinners—who may wish to rotate their assignments. If the party is too small for three cooks, two will do—one for breakfasts and lunches, the other for dinners. Cooks are responsible for camp food supplies and menus.

Water boy. Draws water to maintain ample supply of pure drinking, cooking, and washing water, responsible for purifying water for drinking and cooking.

Dishwasher. Washes and rinses dishes and pots and pans; oils cutlery; keeps cooking equipment clean; responsible for garbage disposal; burns, flattens and buries cans; burns garbage.

Camp maid. Airs sleeping bags and blankets; launders towels, dishtowels, underwear, socks as needed; sweeps out tent; keeps the camp tidy.

Duty list for breaking camp

1. Burn or bury unusable leftovers
2. Roll up sleeping bags
3. Deflate and roll air mattresses
4. Take down and fold tent
5. Fold up all other equipment
6. Fill in garbage pit and latrine
7. Put out fire
8. Load the car

WEATHER GUIDE

The site should catch the breeze, but not be on a crest where strong winds blow. Camp on the windward side of swampy places or thick brush where insects may breed. Winds blow off water and up canyons by day; down canyons and toward water at night. They die down and shift direction as morning sun begins to warm the earth, and again in late afternoon.

Avoid wind gaps—indicated by slanted trunks and heavier growth away from the wind side.

Least wind usually is from 3 to 6 A.M., most wind between 2 and 4 P.M. However on high coastal peaks or in large, deep, straight valleys or canyons the least wind is from 10 to 11 A.M. and 9 to 10 P.M., most wind from 3 to 4 A.M. and 4 to 5 P.M.

When possible, your camp should have an eastern or southeastern exposure to get the early sun, exposed to permit the sun to dry the ground and tents after rain or heavy dew.

Try to locate on the edge of a clearing, with trees between it and the hottest sun of the day. In thick forest, air warms and cools more slowly than in more open spaces.

Cold air and frost flow downward like water and settle in canyon bottoms and low pockets. A low ceiling of canvas or tree branches will keep you warmer when you are sleeping in the open.

Wilderness camping

Camping far from established campgrounds can be a challenge, but it offers many rewards in solitude, open space, unspoiled beauty, and freedom from restrictions found in organized campgrounds. You can apply your cooking and camping skills to a greater degree than in organized areas.

You are, of course, still bound by the same general rules of good sense and conservation as on any public lands. You will also need a campfire permit in most areas.

WHERE TO GO

These wilder lands may be found at high altitudes, on plateaus, in the desert, and on wild beaches.

High country

Wilderness camping in the mountains is not for the novice. Almost all high country camping involves backpacking, which means hiking with a heavy pack on your back, often up steep trails.

Approach this type of camping under the guidance of an experienced backpacker. You can gain experience by several short trips, increasing your challenges as you become more proficient.

High country camping is a specialized kind of camping, not only requiring excellent physical condition, but also demanding specialized techniques and special lightweight equipment.

Some campers prefer to hire a pack animal to carry the heavy equipment. You can also enjoy back country camping by hiring a packer and animals to carry in your equipment and supplies; you can arrange for him to leave you at your base camp and return at a designated time to carry your equipment back to civilization. Complete guide and pack service is also available.

Plateau country

Much of the West is plateau country, ranging between 3,000 and 6,000 feet elevation. In many places it differs little from desert; spaces are vast, with few distinguishing landmarks. You can get lost easily, water is often a problem, and temperature ranges tend to be great. Days may be quite warm, but at night the thermometer drops rapidly.

Plants and trees usually are scattered, and you may have difficulty finding protected places to camp. Your planning must include good maps, an adequate supply of water, and equipment both for sun protection in the daytime and adequate warmth at night. Firewood may be a problem, as on the desert.

Desert

Summer camping on the desert is not for the inexperienced camper; even if you are well equipped and near civilization, the temperature is just too hot and uncomfortable. But from late fall through early spring, the vast deserts of the southwestern United States provide interesting off-season camping.

Camping in the desert requires good maps, an adequate supply of water, and a presumption you will not find much firewood.

Deserts can be pitiless if you get into trouble. Often people still die from dehydration if they get lost, or if their vehicle breaks down or runs out of gasoline. Deep penetrations of both plateau country and desert are best made with two vehicles in company.

Beach

If you camp on a beach, you must be prepared for brilliant sun during the day and cold, damp winds in the evening. You will want to find a spot protected from blowing sand. Moisture usually permeates everything at night.

The damp air may seem chilly, so go prepared with adequate clothing. Rig extra tarpaulins as wind and sun breaks. Even with an entire ocean at your feet, fresh water may not be available; streams should not be used as a water supply unless you can be absolutely sure they are free of pollution.

Use a pair of wet logs to contain your evening campfire. When you leave turn them over and soak them thoroughly, otherwise they might smoulder for days.

WILDERNESS PRECAUTIONS

Whenever you plan to enter rough, unpopulated country, make sure someone in the area knows generally where you are going, and when you expect to get back. In some of the larger parks this is mandatory; you report out and in with the ranger. More than ever, make sure your vehicle is in good working order and that you have a reserve supply of fuel.

If you are lost, or if your vehicle breaks down or gets hopelessly stuck in sand, stay with the vehicle. More fatalities are recorded for those who

---

DESERT CAMPING

Selecting a proper campsite depends a lot on the weather and season. If there is a prevailing wind, try locating your camp on the lee side of high rocks or in a clump of trees, and take along some sort of wind break.

Beware of dry washes, particularly in summer and early fall—they are avenues for flash floods. Locate on high ground near a dry wash to enjoy vegetation and spring wildflowers.

Winter nights are cold in the desert, but the daytime sun is usually warm. Campers in late spring and early fall will usually find a northern exposure best for a cooler daytime camp.

With few exceptions, plan to take your own fuel and water so that you can be independent of the natural supply.

Shelter. Desert conditions are too unreliable for extended, unprotected camping in the open.

The best tent for the desert is a wall tent with a floor in it. The floor helps to keep out sand and desert rodents and insects, and it helps keep the tent warm on a cold winter night. Late spring and early fall campers use a white tent (to reflect the heat) or a tent with a fly or second roof (the air space between fly and tent is insulation). In winter it is a good idea to close up your tent the minute the sun leaves it, to keep in some of the day's warmth.

It's a good idea to sleep on a cot of some kind, off the ground, to avoid desert varmints. Cold nights call for insulation under your sleeping bag.

Water. Transporting water is one of the desert camper's big problems. Most people carry it in 5-gallon jeep cans—easy to handle and store in the car. Two gallons a day per person is the recommended amount. You learn to wash your hands no more than absolutely necessary. A bath is something you postpone until you get home.

For cool water while driving, almost everyone carries a supplementary supply in a water bag on the car bumper.

Food. For the most part you'll have to depend on canned and dried foods, as fresh food does not keep well in the desert. Portable iceboxes are feasible only on weekend jaunts or in a campground near an ice supply.

Keep food in a wood or metal box with a tight-fitting lid to keep out desert animals. Keep the box in the shade.

Cooking and the campfire. Only a novice tries to cook over a campfire in the desert. Winds can make it almost impossible, even if you find or bring enough wood to keep your fire going. Most campers use a gasoline stove.

Campfires are usually built only for nighttime warmth and sociability. It is usually easier to bring fuel from home than to spend long hours scrounging for it in the desert. Never cut desert trees or brush; use only dead wood.

Clothing. The desert's extremes in temperature make a variety of clothing necessary: wool shirts, a wind jacket, and perhaps some coveralls for night use, and cotton clothes for the daytime. You'll also want high-topped boots for hiking; they protect your legs from low-growing brush, cacti, and snakes, and they keep sand and pebbles out of your shoes.

BEACH CAMPING

Camping on the beach provides a pleasant change from the standard vacation in the woods. Here are some pointers when camping near the ocean.

Make sure that the site you select is available for camping. Many miles of ocean frontage are privately owned, or belong to cities with ordinances against beach camping. Inquire locally before you make camp. Often you can rent space from the owner of a private beach.

Check tide tables and study the beach evidence to determine where and when high tide will come, and make camp well outside its reach.

Explore the surrounding area to learn if there are any tide pools or marshy spots that harbor mosquitoes; if so, drive on to another site. Take mosquito netting and insect repellents.

Shelter and equipment. Be prepared for strong winds. Pitch your tent with its back to the ocean or quartered into the wind. If possible, guy the tent. Use extra-long stakes, or bury stakes or chunks of driftwood under at least a foot of sand and tie them to the stake loops. Carry a windbreak.

If your tent has a buiit-in floor, it will need protection because of the yielding nature of the sand beneath it. Put down a piece of plywood over the area where you walk.

If your camp is not visible from the surf, place a marker near it that can be seen from the ocean.

Otherwise you may have trouble finding it if you wander down the beach.

Salt air corrodes aluminum, so cover aluminum pots and utensils when not in use. Keep a light coating of oil or paraffin on the aluminum zippers on the tent, sleeping bags, or duffel bags to keep them from sticking.

Cooking and fuel. Don't rely entirely on a wood fire for cooking; wind currents are often unpredictable. A gasoline stove is more reliable and it can be shifted to avoid the wind.

In some localities you will have to cart in your own firewood. Driftwood is plentiful on northern beaches, but is scarce in southern latitudes.

Water. Be prepared to carry your own water; take along two or three 5-gallon cans or bottles that you can fill at a service station.

Your car. Salt air and wind-driven sand can dull the finish of your car and may cause exposed parts to corrode or rust. Keep car covered with a tarp.

Take along a shovel, and tire chains or gunny sacks, to be used if the wheels get stuck in sand. If the car gets stuck, dig out a ramp for the rear wheels to climb, and line it with brush, planking, or gunny sacks. Tire chains can be laid flat on the sand in front of the wheels for traction.

---

bravely volunteer to go for help than for those who stay behind and wait.

Three columns of smoke is a distress signal, and don't be reluctant to use the signal if you need help. Smoke signals can be seen a long distance in clear air and open country, and a helicopter can get to you in minutes. Make your fires at least 10 yards apart, or distance may make them merge into one to the viewer.

You should be more cautious than usual about varmints; you are more apt to encounter an occasional rattlesnake, particularly in the cool of the evening on the plateaus and deserts. In the desert there are scorpions, centipedes, and Gila monsters. Shake your sleeping bag out at night as a safety precaution, and turn your shoes upside down and shake them each morning.

THE CAMPSITE

Most of the basic rules apply. Try to determine the prevailing wind, and back your tent into it, consistent with other good orientation such as drainage and convenience. If the soil is very light and sandy, you may need extra long tent stakes.

Remember that sudden local storms can strike in plateau and desert country, just as in the mountains, and floods are worse where there is no vegetation to hold them back.

Building a fireplace

You will probably have to make your own fireplace at an unimproved campsite. The safest and most convenient spot is on bare ground where you have room to work and where no overhead branches will be ignited. If no bare spot exists, clear away the forest duff with a shovel, scraping a 10-foot circle down to bare earth. Be sure you do not expose any roots where you plan to build your fire, because they can carry fire underground.

Choose a slight rise to insure drainage away from the fire. Build your fireplace with two parallel rows of rocks set at least 2 feet apart, or use two short thick lengths of logs. (The latter will last several days before they burn up.) Line up the rocks or logs so the prevailing wind passes between them and away from the cooking end. Rest your fire irons, grill, or hot plate on top. (Avoid wet or stratified rocks—they may explode when heated.)

KEYHOLE FIREPLACE lined with rocks has fire built in large end, coals scraped into smaller end for cooking.

Latrine

If you must provide your own sanitary facilities, select a secluded spot, downhill from camp, at least 100 feet from the cooking fire, and remote from the source of drinking water.

Dig a hole or trench at least 2 feet deep and pile the dirt alongside. Screen for privacy with tarpaulins, old sheets, boughs, or whatever you can find. As the pit is used, dirt should be shoveled in and chlorinated lime sprinkled into it. When it is half filled, fill in with soil and dig a new pit.

Some car campers carry a knocked-down toilet seat and rack, which folds for transporting and can be assembled in camp; others improvise with the stray pieces of packing case or tree branches they find on the site. Portable toilets with disposable plastic bags are available in sporting goods stores and by mail.

Garbage pit

In unimproved camping areas you will need to dig a pit for burying bottles and burned and flattened cans. Garbage should be burned rather than buried, because it attracts insects and animals. Buried garbage is easily detected by roving animals and dug out with mystifying noises in the dead of night.

Drinking water

Campers who favor remote sites, far from piped water, should take precautions to avoid dysentery,

typhus, and other water-borne diseases.

The simplest method for purifying water is to boil it for at least 5 minutes. To get rid of the flat taste, aerate it by pouring back and forth several times from one container to another. If the water has an unpleasant flavor, boil it with charcoal from the campfire for 15 minutes and let it stand overnight. Strain it through cloth.

Quicker results can be obtained by adding Halazone tablets to the water (2 to a quart; let stand 30 minutes), but the resulting flavor is far from thirst-quenching.

COOKING

For easy cooking you should have a grill large enough to go over the fire. Many campers carry several lengths of reinforcing steel rods or a piece of expanded metal. You can also purchase grills with folding legs.

Your fire

Cooking will be somewhat different than in an organized campground. If your group is small, you may confine your cooking to a camp stove. (In a few parks no campfires are allowed.) Unless you have adequate firewood, your fire will be smaller, and you must cook quickly before it dies down.

Many people take small braziers, possibly a Japanese hibachi, with them into areas where firewood is scarce. A sizable bag of charcoal will cook quite a few meals. Other campers use pressed sawdust logs pre-split into one-inch sections.

When rocks and adequate firewood are available, the best fireplace for cooking is the keyhole, particularly if you are cooking with several utensils. You build it pretty much in the shape of a keyhole, with a narrow end and wider circular end. The fire is built in the larger section, then coals are scraped into the narrow end for a hot steady cooking fire.

True campfire cooking

One of the good things about camping away from organized areas is that you have much more latitude in cooking. You won't have a convenient, waist-level fireplace, but a real campfire. Reflector oven cooking can be done only with a campfire, and to do pit and Dutch oven cookery you must dig some holes. This, of course, is severely frowned on in organized campgrounds.

You can make beanhole beans and bake ham or fish in the ground that will taste better than anything you can cook at home, especially with the open air to give you an appetite. On the beaches you can easily dig pits and gather wet seaweed for an old-fashioned clambake.

Pit cooking. The accepted version of rock-lined pit construction is as follows:

Dig a hole about three times as large as the food you are going to cook. Slope the sides of the pit a little. Line the bottom and sides with rocks, choosing flat ones which will not tend to roll down to the bottom. Build a fire in the pit and let it burn briskly for 3 or 4 hours, or until the pit is filled with hot coals. Shovel out the coals and pour a quart of water over the sizzling hot stones.

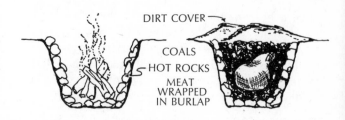

Place a thick layer of leaves (cabbage, corn, wild grape, maple, seaweed, or any sweet leaves) over the hot stones. Then place your meat or fish, which should be wrapped in a number of layers of brown paper or parchment paper, then in wet burlap, and then fastened with wire. Cover with more leaves; add vegetables or fruit (wrapped in leaves) and more leaves; then a layer of hot coals. Cover with wet burlap and earth to seal in the heat and steam.

There are a few precautions. Be sure the hole and rocks are really hot, and that your food is well protected from scorching and from the taste of such protective wrappings as damp burlap (which adds nothing at all to the flavor). Generally, the longer things are cooked in the hole the better. For a large amount of food, three to four hours should be enough. A chicken with potatoes and corn in a small hole should be ready in two hours.

Some experts advise wrapping the cloth-covered food in four thicknesses of damp news-

---

HOW TO USE AN AX

TO CUT BRANCHES

CHOP HERE

NEVER HERE

PUT WEIGHT ON THIS END FOR SAFETY

NO → ← YES

TO CHOP BRANCH OFF FALLEN TREE, CHOP TOWARD TREE TOP

TO CUT LOGS

THICKNESS OF LOG

A C B
D

CHOP FROM SIDE HALFWAY THROUGH LOG, THEN CHOP FROM OTHER SIDE *OR* CHOP OUT KERFS A AND B, SPLIT OUT PIECE C, THEN CHOP OUT KERF D

paper. This holds heat better, and the cloth will not get brown spots on it from the coals or rocks.

Do not leave any campfire—even a buried one—unattended. Fire can travel underground, along dead tree roots, for example. Be sure it is out before you leave it.

Dutch oven cookery. Camp cooks skilled in the use of a Dutch oven claim it is a better oven than your kitchen oven, capable of producing better food. The preferred kind for outdoor use is large and heavy, with 3 legs to stand on and a slightly concave cover on which coals may be heaped. A regular cover may be used if it is inverted. If your Dutch oven has no legs, improvise a way to rest the bottom on rocks; direct contact with the coals may scorch your dinner. The greatest danger with a Dutch oven lies in getting the inside temperature too high, but a little practice will show you how to regulate the coals on top and on the ground below it.

The Dutch oven is used to sear meats quickly and then bring out their tenderness by long, slow cooking, as for a pot roast or stew. It can be used for beans, fricasseed chicken, casseroles, stews, and clam chowder. The Dutch oven can also be used for baking cornbread, biscuits, sourdough, cakes, and pies.

EARTH

ASHES AND COALS

EARTH

ASHES AND COALS

In pit cooking with a Dutch oven, a dry heat is needed. No leaves or burlap are used and coals, drawn from the bottom of the hole, are heaped on top of the oven.

Dig a pit a little larger than the oven, build a fire in the pit, and let the fire burn until you have a good bed of glowing coals. Shovel out most of the coals, put the Dutch oven containing the food into the pit, and shovel the coals back in around and on top of the oven. Place dirt or sand over the top so that the heat will be regulated and the food won't burn.

In campfire Dutch oven cooking, the bottom heat is regulated by covering the coals around the oven with dirt. In like manner, the coals exposed to the air on top of the lid may give too much heat unless ashes or dirt are added. With an open fire, a good bed of coals is essential. In some localities and with certain woods, you may need a separate fire from which you can borrow coals.

Reflector oven cooking. This cleverly designed camping accessory can do almost anything that the home oven can do—bake pie, gingerbread, coffee cake, cornbread, biscuits, and muffins; cook casseroles; broil bacon, trout, or steaks.

The oven is scientifically designed so the sharply sloped and highly polished top and bottom of the oven focus heat from the fire on a central point—a baking pan. To do a good job, the oven must be kept shiny.

Reflector ovens may be purchased in camp supply stores; they generally come in two sizes—12 and 16 inches wide. They fold into a flat, compact package that fits easily into the camp outfit. Being made of aluminum, they are quite light in weight—1½ to 2 pounds.

A reflector fire of hardwood is the best source of baking heat. Avoid pitchy woods that produce smoke which could spoil the flavor of your prize recipe if the smoke is blown into the open-faced oven.

The oven should be placed so that the reflected heat from the fire will reach the food. Build the fire against a back log or back rock, and place the oven on the opposite side of the fire. Keep the fire burning continuously at about the same intensity during the entire cooking period. Heat above and below the food should be approximately equal, surrounding the pot with uniform heat. Turn the pot as necessary for even cooking.

The optimum distance between the oven and the fire will depend on the size and intensity of the fire and on the type of food being cooked. Experience—good old trial and error—will be your best guide.

For baking loaf bread or cake, which require more time, it is well to build a separate baking fire and add a few sticks to it occasionally as you go about your other culinary tasks.

Use hot pads or gloves to move the oven closer to or farther from the fire. Turn it slightly to accomplish even browning.

Biscuits, cornbread, muffins, scalloped dishes, macaroni and cheese, and even chicken broilers, can be cooked successfully in a reflector oven. Many packaged mixes can be used successfully in a reflector oven. The cooking time will be a little longer than in a regular oven.

Camping with children

Camping is tremendous fun for most youngsters, but a little advance planning certainly makes life easier. Where you go and the kind of camping you will do depends to a great extent on the ages and interests of the children.

Very small tots are usually happiest if they can play on a long sloping beach. Children from 6 to 12 enjoy improved campgrounds with other families around, with plenty of playmates and a place to swim. Older children may enjoy the challenge of wilderness camping, or they may prefer gregarious camps where boating and water-skiing are available.

CLOTHING

To a child, one of the joys of camping is being able to get wet and dirty as often as he likes. Plenty of durable old shoes and clothing is the rule; jeans and flannel shirts or T-shirts are standard. Sneakers are ideal to wear around camp—comfortable, inexpensive, and washable.

You will want to pack swim suits, and plenty of warm outer clothing for evenings or unexpected cold. Be sure to bring rain wear for them; sudden showers won't dampen their enthusiasm.

ON THE WAY

Children get restless on a long trip, so plan ahead to make the trip a delight instead of a trial.

Keep them comfortable. Pack your gear in the car so that the smaller ones can see out (build up the back seat with sleeping bags or blankets), move around a bit, or nap. Use suitcases and other objects to build up the floor space in the back of the car so that it is level with the seat. Some station wagon campers make a second floor out of plywood and mount it in the back compartment below the windows. Camp gear is stowed below it and a mattress on top makes a bed.

Keep the children entertained. Toys and picture books, and even simple guessing games, will appeal to young children. School-age children love car games—identifying license plates or automobiles, Twenty Questions, I Spy, and other guessing games.

Stop often so they can stretch their legs. A five-minute stop every couple of hours, along with regular comfort-station stops, will let them work off childish energies. Lunch should be a longer

SMALL CHILDREN will enjoy digging in the sand with pail and shovel. Also bring a favorite toy or two.

TAKING THE BABY

With the versatile baby equipment and disposable items now available, taking the baby camping is no longer the chore it once was. Now more families are doing it as a matter of course.

Here are a few pointers:

1. Check with your family doctor before you go, and camp within range of a doctor. (Rangers are trained to give first aid.)

2. If you plan to use dry formula at camp, get the baby on it well ahead of time.

3. A change in water may upset the baby; bring a gallon or two from home to last through the first few days. Camp water may have a high mineral content, so you may want to use distilled water for formula during the entire stay.

4. Be sure to bring enough canned baby food. Find out in advance if you can replenish the supply locally.

5. Disposable diapers will lighten your daily work load.

6. Washing or rinsing diapers in lakes or streams is illegal; it pollutes the water. Rinse diapers, soak in a pail overnight with diaper soap, then put them through several hot rinses next morning.

7. Avoid spraying insect poisons around the baby or his things. Use mosquito netting to protect him while he sleeps.

You'll want to consider taking along some of the following for your baby:

Bed-carriage with removable wheels

Combination playpen and crib

Car seat

Car bed (under 6 months)

Collapsible playpen

Bottle warmer which plugs into car lighter

Back carrier—several types available; some make into a car seat and high chair

BACK CARRIERS let you go hiking with infants. Frame distributes weight evenly for comfort.

break. A relaxed schedule prevents arguments and fussing brought on by fatigue. If time permits, make brief stops along the way at children's museums, playgrounds, or swimming pools. Adults, if too intent on getting to the destination, may overlook the trip itself as a source of pleasure for children.

Bring milk or juice in a thermos and crackers and fruit to quench thirst and still hunger pangs between meals. Sweets should be avoided if possible, as the motion of the car combined with too many sweets sometimes upsets small stomachs. Carry a dampened washcloth or two in a plastic bag, or tuck in some disposable pre-moistened paper towels for wiping off sticky hands and faces.

If the children are prone to car sickness, have your doctor prescribe motion-sickness tablets for them to take and have a few paper bags on hand for emergencies. Be sure they get plenty of fresh air. It sometimes helps a car-sick child if you let him ride in the front seat for awhile.

IN CAMP

Once you reach camp, you seldom have to worry about keeping children amused. The new surroundings will interest them, and in most camping areas they will find playmates among other camping families.

The whole family should explore the campsite vicinity soon after arrival so that all will know what activities are available, what places must be avoided, and what precautions are necessary.

Set up a few camp rules (most of which are common sense or good manners): To stay within the confines of the campsite and out of other

BLUEPRINT PAPER from drafting supply store retains patterns when exposed in sun. Develop in cold water.

TAKING PETS TO CAMP

Some campgrounds do not allow pets; others do, but specify that pets must be kept on a leash, under owner's control, or confined in a vehicle.

At night animals must remain inside a tent or vehicle. Some parks do not allow animals on trails. Pets are not allowed to stay in camp if they are noisy, vicious, dangerous, or disturbing to others.

If you are going to take your pet to camp, you must plan for him as for another member of the family. He will need utensils, food, grooming tools, and shelter if accustomed to it.

A pet who seldom rides in an automobile must go through a training period. Let him sit in the parked car a few times. Then take him on short trips. Ask your vet what you can give him to prevent car sickness. Don't give him food for several hours before leaving, and very little water. You can give him small amounts of water along the way, but refrain from feeding until you've finished the day's traveling. Stop and let your pet out occasionally, but keep him on a leash.

Pets should not be leashed by the collar in the car; they can jump out an open window and break their necks or strangle. Nor should pets be left in a closed car, particularly in the sun. Leave two windows partially open on opposite sides for cross ventilation, and park in the shade if possible.

If you are taking a dog over state lines, be sure you have a certificate showing a rabies vaccination within the past 6 months. Some states require it.

people's camps; not to litter, either in or out of camp; never to destroy or damage natural life or features. Teach them to recognize poison ivy or poison oak and to stay away from it. Make them understand the dangers of approaching too close to wild animals.

Assign a few chores to each child old enough to help, and remember to rotate chores later. All except the very young should take care of personal gear. Children can gather firewood, help build the fire, try their hand at camp cooking and setting up equipment.

Nature pastimes

Many state and federal campgrounds offer nature hikes conducted by a ranger-naturalist. Children—and adults—will enjoy learning about the plant and animal life near their camping area. Many parks have natural history museums and booklets about the area.

Children enjoy exploring, identifying, and collecting (check for restrictions), and some may enjoy keeping a nature scrapbook or notebook. Inexpensive pocket books are available to help them in identification of regional birds, trees, flowers, insects, and animals; stars and constellations; rocks and shells.

You can also teach children how to blaze trails with rocks and forked sticks; older children may want to learn to read trail maps or use a compass.

Quiet-time projects in camp can include crafts using materials from nature. You can do a variety of printing projects using leaves, shells, seed pods, ferns. Use a water-base paint or colored stamp pads for easy clean-up. Making blueprints with shells, leaves and ferns appeals to many youngsters. You will find ideas for camp crafts in *Crafts for Children* (Lane Books, Menlo Park, Calif., 1968; $1.95).

Fun in camp

Younger children should have a favorite toy or two in camp, as well as games, story books, puzzles, and coloring materials. Older ones will enjoy reading, drawing, and table games in the evenings for a change of pace.

Provide incentive for them to help keep the camp clean; you might suggest collecting and making a chain of beverage can rings, with a prize

TIN CAN STOVE is practical for children learning to cook. Punch vents in large can, use tin snips to trim out section for fire tending. For cooking use small pan or coffee can with wire handle.

for the child with the longest chain at the end of your stay.

Outdoor cooking

Many children learn the rudiments of outdoor cookery through organized groups or at a summer camp. These supervised lessons are just a start, and during a camping trip they might like to do some outdoor cooking on their own.

If you would like to help your children learn more about outdoor cooking, here are some suggestions for cooking projects for small groups of children, from ages 7 to 16. The cooking skills that children can handle depend on their previous experience. As parents, you can guide them to try techniques within their abilities.

Outdoor cooking for children follows a logical succession: planning meals, building and tending a fire, organizing equipment, cooking on a stick, mastering one-pot cookery, frying-pan cookery, foil cookery, barbecuing, and taking responsibility for cleanup. More advanced skills include baking in a reflector oven and in a bean hole.

You can find recipes for simple dishes in Scouting manuals or booklets published by organized youth groups. Group leaders have found the following cooking techniques successful with both boys and girls of different ages.

Ages 7, 8. Fire building, cooking cocoa, toasting bread for sandwiches, and making S'mores. This age is very eager, but impatient. They are competent to carry out simple, one-step projects.

Ages 9 to 11. Stick cookery, such as Bread Twists; all kinds of kebabs, breakfasts, one-pot meals, and cooking over tin can stoves. This age still does not have patience with foods that cook slowly.

Ages 12 to 14 (Junior high). Barbecuing; plank cooking; hot rock cookery; and foil cookery of individual stews, baked potatoes, and baked apples. Younger children will find foil cookery difficult; it is hard for them to judge the heat of the fire and tell when the food is cooked.

Ages 15, 16. Reflector oven cooking of gingerbread, biscuits, fruit cobbler, bean hole cookery.

Keeping track of children

Impress children that if they do get lost, to stay in one place until found. Some parents pin identification badges on the youngest children or give each child a whistle to blow if lost.

If the older ones are hiking by themselves, set an alarm clock and put it in one of their knapsacks to remind them to start back to camp.

Tips for novice hikers

Many campgrounds are surrounded by a network of well-marked trails, leading to fishing streams, swimming holes, or scenic attractions or views. Some parks have short nature walks.

Day hikes away from camp are fun, as you can take time to enjoy the interesting details of nature close up. But don't be too ambitious at first, unless you are in good physical condition.

EQUIPMENT

Campers who take to the trails on short hikes should consider acquiring a small amount of desirable equipment. Here are a few suggestions for articles which might increase your enjoyment:

Knapsack. A small canvas knapsack will provide you with a comfortable way to carry lunch, camera, film, fishing tackle, and an extra sweater on the trail.

Canteen. If water may be a problem, carry at least a 1-quart canteen. You may want to carry a cup.

Pocket first aid kit. Make up your own kit with some band-aids, a small roll of 2-inch adhesive tape, razor blade, antiseptic, matches in waterproof container, a chapstick, and possibly a snake bite kit.

Compass. A pocket compass is helpful in orienting yourself to your map and in getting back to camp if you are lost. (Look backward occasionally on your way out.)

Trail map. Even though trails near improved camping grounds are well marked, you may want to carry a detailed map of the area. Rangers sometimes can provide one, but serious explorers will want to buy U.S.G.S. topographic maps.

Other things you may want to include: dark glasses, bandanas, extra socks, pocket knife, flashlight, required drugs, lunch and snack foods.

GENERAL RULES OF TRAIL TRAVEL

Following are some of the basic rules of hiking:

1. Don't hike alone. For security reasons, travel in groups, or at least in pairs. If one member of the party sprains an ankle or becomes ill on the trail, the other can go for help. With three in the party, one can remain with the injured person.

2. Tell someone where you are going and when you expect to return. Be specific. If you get lost or injured, friends will know where to look for you.

3. Set a comfortable, steady pace you can keep up. A conservative pace eats up the miles without exhausting you.

4. Let the slowest hiker lead or walk near the front; put the fastest in the rear. In this way, the fast hikers will not leave the slowpokes behind. In a large party, split into two groups—fast and slow; each group can set its own pace, but agree on a rendezvous point.

5. Keep track of the time. Take a watch so you can allow sufficient time to return to camp before dark. Check time needed to reach your destination, and allow at least as much time (or more) to return.

6. Take it easy ascending steep slopes. A slow, methodical pace can get you up the hill without panting. Zigzag trails are easier to climb than vertical ones.

7. Wear low boots and heavy socks. Clothing should be loose and comfortable. Go easy on exposing yourself until you have acquired a good, deep tan. Wear a hat if hiking in the sun for a long period.

8. To ford a stream, take off shoes and socks. If your feet are too tender, wear shoes without socks and put the socks back on after you've crossed the stream.

9. Stop heel blisters from forming by covering chafed spots with adhesive tape. If blisters form, wash and cover with a large square of adhesive tape without gauze. Leave alone for 5 days. Keep socks wrinkle-free.

10. To aid digestion on the trail, start off slowly, take a siesta after lunch, and rest before dinner. Avoid fatty foods for breakfast or lunch. Eat a light lunch and drink plenty of water. If you perspire freely, add salt to your food.

11. Don't trust the water (except piped) along well-traveled trails. Carry a canteen of pure water or water-purifying tablets.

12. Pack and saddle stock have the right-of-way at all times on the trails. Packers accompanying the stock may suggest the best place for you to stand. Remain quiet and stationary while the animals are passing.

13. Taking short cuts on switchbacks is a dangerous practice that is prohibited in national forests and parks. Dislodged rocks are hazardous for hikers downtrail, and short cuts often erode in the rainy season and cause washouts.

14. If you require a campfire, build it in a safe place and completely extinguish it before you leave. Use no more wood than you actually need.

15. If you leave the trail to explore, do not take chances. Lack of caution is the principal cause of wilderness and fishing injuries.

16. If you think you are lost, take it easy. Sit down and try to figure out where you are. If night is coming on, make camp instead of trying to find your way back. Remember the international distress signal of three, repeated at intervals—three shots, lights, shouts, fires, smoke signals, pieces of white clothing—anything that can be seen or heard from a distance. Try not to worry—if you don't reason your way back, you'll probably be found soon enough.

17. Leave a clean camp. Refuse left behind will attract wild animals and will destroy the natural beauty for the next camper. Carry your leftovers out with you, or burn and bury them.

18. If your hike takes you through settled country, observe no-trespassing signs, leave all gates as you find them, do not disturb pastured stock.

FOOTWEAR

Proper footwear can make the difference between an enjoyable vacation and one of misery. Whether your hiking is confined to walking along paths to

DAY HIKES away from camp are fun. Pick a trail according to your ability, and take along lunch in a knapsack.

scenic points or expanded to hike along mountain trails, your feet deserve the best of care.

For light hiking, you can wear any flat-heeled camp shoes. Even on short walks, however, high-topped shoes keep out gravel and sand.

Feet expand in size as you hike, especially on a long trip over rough terrain. If a shoe or boot is either tight or poorly constructed, it can't take this expansion and general discomfort results. Boots must allow ample room for wiggling toes freely, but be snug enough to prevent chafing. *Break in boots thoroughly at home before you start.*

Hiking boots. All leather, 6 to 8-inch boots are considered best for trail and cross-country wear. Leather should be soft and pliable, and stretch to fit the foot. Soles should be made of cleated rubber or composition to stand trail abuse.

Take good care of your boots. Choose a dressing that complements natural leather oils. Shoe polish wax is the best water repellent. Dry boots by stuffing with wads of newspaper, which blot up moisture. Hang boots by laces from a branch or rod so they will dry all over.

Socks. For all serious hiking, wear two pairs of socks. Many hikers wear a cotton pair next to the skin, with an outer pair of wool which absorbs perspiration and holds warmth. Two pairs of socks will pad the space between foot and boot, provide insulation in cold weather.

Handling the unexpected...

You cannot drag some people camping. They look upon a stay in the woods as a perilous adventure, with every night an old-time Hallowe'en. They see themselves cooking in the rain, warding off clouds of mosquitoes, emptying snakes out of sleeping bags, and defending their supplies from bears, deer, porcupines, and Gila monsters.

Of course no one camper has such a busy time of it. Occasionally you may have to outsmart a hungry bear, or a shower forces you inside the tent. More often you have to fight off mosquitoes and other flying pests. But most campers have no real trouble.

The plain fact that you *might* meet a bear or a snake, however, points up the desirability of knowing how to cope with unfamiliar situations and emergencies that can conceivably occur.

RAINSTORM

If it might rain, take a few precautionary measures:

Advance preparations. Ditch around the tent, spread a canvas fly above the cooking-dining area, store foods in a dry spot (tent or car), keep a supply of wet-weather fire-starting materials under shelter, put rain clothes inside the tent, keep extra water-proofed coverings at hand. If you leave camp for a few hours, move exposed bedding into tent, cover cooking gear with a waterproof sheet.

If caught unprepared. If your bedding is soaked, you may just as well pack up for home or the nearest guest cabin, because it will take at least several days for your bedding to dry (unless you find a laundromat with automatic dryers nearby).

If bedding and clothes are dry, you can salvage your stay with some of these measures: Rig a tarp or poncho over the cooking area to shield fire and cook (take tarp down as soon as rain stops). Eat inside tent or car. Or move inside the tent, and cook and eat there.

To keep the tent clean, cover the floor with loose brush and place a brush doormat in front of the tent as a boot-wipe. Roll up sleeping bags during the day and stack out of the way, or cover with tarps for seats. Loosen tent and tarp ropes.

When the rain stops, dry wet clothes over the campfire. Cut a green pole about 6 feet long and set it in position with one end 4 or 5 feet above the fire, the other driven into the soil. Loop the

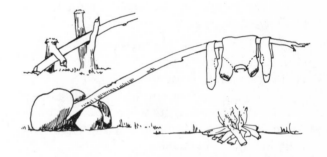

wet clothes over the end above the fire and keep a low, flameless fire going until the soaked things are dry. Or hang on a clothesline near the fire.

Break out the playing cards, puzzles, paperback books, whittling knife, or the harmonica, and relax inside the tent or car until the storm departs.

WINDSTORM

Chief casualties of a windstorm will be your canvas goods, but if staunchly roped, they should come through in good shape.

Guy your tent if possible, or if you are not using the tent, collapse it until the wind dies down. Hold down tarpaulin or plastic coverings with rocks; fold up canvas chairs and cots; drown your campfire to prevent embers from being scattered into the forest.

LIGHTNING STORM

If you are not used to it, lightning can be a scary experience in the mountains, but the chances of its coming anywhere near you are so remote that you might as well enjoy the spectacular display. You should, however, stay off high, exposed areas and away from isolated trees.

FOREST FIRE

Campers have little to fear from forest fire. If your campground lies in the path of a fire, you will be notified in plenty of time to break camp and get your family to safety. When fire hazard is high, some campgrounds are closed.

Keep a shovel and several gallons of water near your campfire at all times. Instruct your children in fire safety and emergency procedures.

Campfire safety. Always practice fire safety in your campsite. Hold used matches in your hand until they are completely out, then break them in two. Do not throw cigarettes, cigar butts, or pipe heels on the dry forest floor; clear a space down to mineral soil and grind out the fire with your foot.

Keep gasoline and other flammable liquids away from your campsite, and always put them away before starting a fire. Never keep gasoline in your tent. Gasoline should not be stored in glass, which magnifies the sun and also may break.

Extinguish campfires with plenty of water and mineral earth. Soak the burning embers, stirring water into them with a stick, until you are sure every spark is dead. Feel among the coals with your bare hand; cover the dead coals with earth.

Never leave your campfire unattended even for a short time. Many a camper has lost his whole outfit through such carelessness—and started a serious fire as well.

If a fire breaks out in your camp, fight it yourself without delay. Shovel dirt and dump water on it. If necessary, smother it with blankets—your insurance company will replace them. Notify the ranger immediately. Scatter baking soda or dirt on a cooking fire, dirt on a gasoline or kerosene one.

Fighting forest fires. One of your duties as a citizen is to fight forest fires if ordered to do so, but your chances of joining a fire line are remote. Forest authorities can call upon hundreds of trained fire fighters; however your help might be required with rear-echelon duties.

FREEZING WEATHER

If you are camping in a high-altitude campground, particularly in early summer or fall, you should go prepared for freezing weather.

Advance preparations. Be sure the car cooling system is filled with anti-freeze, the battery charged up (a low battery will freeze), and chains are packed. Take along extra blankets or woolen sleeping-bag liners, stocking caps, mittens, and mufflers; pack plenty of newspapers for insulation.

If caught unprepared. Drain the car radiator, engine block, and heater. Move freezable supplies into the tent, or store in your insulated chest.

If sleeping on cots, shift to the ground. Spread layers of newspaper under and over sleeping bags. Zip mated bags together and sleep double.

Heat the tent with gasoline stove or lantern or Dutch oven filled with coals; remember to provide ventilation. Or build a reflecting fire that will throw heat into the tent, and open the front of the tent to receive the heat. If you are sleeping in the open, pitch a canvas fly above the sleeping bags at an angle to capture heat from the fire.

WILD ANIMALS

In many parks and forests, wild animals are both fascinating and a camp nuisance.

Bears may haunt the roads, cadging handouts from motorists, and roam the camp after dark, seeking food.

Shy and tame as they look, deer are wild creatures and should be treated with respect. Be particularly wary of does with fawns. If the deer becomes frightened or angry, it may slash at you with its razor-sharp front hoofs. Don't feed them; their digestive systems can't absorb human food.

Porcupines are stubborn, anti-social little beasts that like to forage and are not easily dissuaded from their search. They are particularly fond of salt, and will eat anything that has salt deposited on it from perspiration. To get a porcupine to depart, don't approach too closely, but try lights, noise, a long prod, a well-aimed bucket of water.

Raccoons are especially resourceful thieves, and a big one can quickly dispatch a sizable dog.

SNAKES AND LIZARDS

Almost everyone is afraid of snake bite, especially if he is unfamiliar with the out-of-doors. While you will probably camp for summer after summer and never see a poisonous snake, be sure members of your party are aware of how to avoid them.

Rattlesnakes. Most campers will never see a rattlesnake, in fact, the snake tries to avoid people. It attacks only if surprised, hurt, or cornered. If you hear its rattled warning, jump away from it; usually it will crawl off. But occasionally one strikes without warning.

Be alert and know the rattlesnake's habits. It likes to warm its cold blood on sunny slopes with rocky ledges and sandy stretches. It avoids damp places except at mid-day, and it seldom moves around at night. They are usually found below 6,000 feet, but have been seen as high as 10,000 feet.

About 98 per cent of all snake bites occur below the knee, or on the hand or forearm. More than half of these result from stepping on or too close to a snake; another quarter result from picking up objects near an unseen snake. Hiking boots and heavy, denim trousers provide good protection.

In snake areas, stick to the trails. Look carefully before bending to pick up anything, or in climbing cliffs or ledges.

For the snake bite victim, the best treatment is with antiserum, but it should be administered only by a physician.

Get the patient to a doctor or a hospital as soon as possible. If you can do so within an hour, forget first aid remedies. Transport the patient with as little exertion as possible, doing everything possible to slow down circulation of the poisoned blood. Keep him relaxed, avoid pressing or moving the bitten part, and do not give him alcohol or stimulants. Ice applied to the arm or leg, or soaking it in icy water, helps slow circulation.

If you are far from medical help, you will need to use your snake bite kit. Hikers in snake country should learn the procedure before the trip. But get the patient to a doctor just as soon as possible.

If you can do so without danger, take the dead snake to the doctor; it may not be a rattler.

Desert reptiles. The Arizona desert harbors an unsavory pair of reptiles you'll want to avoid.

The relatively rare coral snake, whose venom is particularly virulent, can be identified by its bright red, yellow, and black rings. It is small and shy, and is seldom encountered in daytime.

The only poisonous lizard is the Gila monster, which is also found in southern Nevada and Utah, and in New Mexico. This lethargic creature is not dangerous unless molested; then it moves swiftly. The Gila monster can be identified by its bead-like scales marked with spots or bands ranging in color from pink to orange.

INSECTS AND OTHER PESTS

Insects are more of an annoyance to the camper than snakes. Many are irritating and their bites can bring discomfort. Some children react strongly to insect bites and may need medical attention.

Flying insects. Take along insect repellent for mosquitoes, flies, gnats, and no-see-ums. To relieve itching, apply a thick paste of baking soda and water, a pack of wet salt, or vinegar in water (1 teaspoon per glass). If severely bitten, drink milk to neutralize the poison, and take antihistamine pills.

Wood tick. In some areas, these are the most troublesome of all the woodland pests, particularly the variety that transmits Rocky Mountain spotted fever and other fevers. Ticks are small, reddish-brown bugs with whitish markings. They cling to the undersides of leaves, to brush, branches, and logs. They can drop on hikers walking through the forest, or become attached to persons sitting on an infected log.

If you discover one on yourself, examine your clothes carefully to see if more are hiding in them. Shake clothing out over newspapers so you can see the ticks when they drop.

The wood tick buries its head in your skin—painlessly. It should never be yanked out because the head will remain embedded and become infected. Remove a tick by grasping it gently but firmly with tweezers or a facial tissue. Pull it out slowly and gently. Make sure no part was left under the skin, then paint the area with antiseptic. If any headache or fever symptoms appear within the next few days, check your physician at once.

Scorpion. This amber-colored translucent arachnid has a stinger at the end of its long tail. Most scorpions in the west are not dangerous to humans, but the sting is painful and causes a welt similar to a wasp sting. Treat with baking soda paste.

Two small species found mainly in the Arizona desert are potentially dangerous, and their sting should be treated just like a snake bite.

Children often react strongly to scorpion bites and should receive medical treatment.

Black widow spider. Rarely encountered, you can identify this spider by a red hourglass on its underside. Their bite is vicious and should be treated like a snake bite. Medical attention is essential. The main sympton is intense abdominal pain a half hour after the person has been bitten.

HOW TO BEHAVE AROUND BEARS

Bears are not dangerous if you leave them alone and stay clear of them. The three main rules in dealing with bears: Don't feed them. Don't get too close to them. Don't argue with them if they decide they want your lunch. Usually harmless, they can be extremely dangerous if crossed.

The grizzly bear, *Ursus horribilis*, is now almost extinct in the United States, but may be encountered in Yellowstone and Glacier national parks, Alaska, and remote parts of Canada. Grizzlies are big, unpredictable, and mean—they may attack without warning or provocation.

The black bear, *Ursus americanus*, is our only native bear, and is common in the wilder areas of the country. More timid and less dangerous than the grizzly, he occasionally turns on people if they startle him or if he thinks they are withholding food handouts.

Bears that enter a campground are drawn by the foods they find around places where humans camp. The hungry bear is unbelievably single-minded in his quest for food. He has an exceedingly keen sense of smell, and if tantalized by a scent, will search with a vengeance—even ripping open a car or camp ice chest or entering a tent in his search. *Never keep anything in a tent that a bear might consider edible*; one ate 25 pounds of axle grease several winters ago, and occasionally one licks the cold cream off a sleeping camper's face!

They are extremely dangerous if startled, frightened, confused, or frustrated; a mother bear with cubs is the most dangerous of all. They are extremely powerful—pound for pound, much stronger than the average man.

To foil bears, pack foods attractive to them—ham, bacon, salt pork, honey—in an airtight container (such as a pressure cooker) and seal to lock in the scent. Or wrap these foods for night storage in several layers of aluminum foil. Hang foods high in the air from the branch of a tree; tie the rope high up the trunk. Don't hang food close to your sleeping area. Dispose of any desirable garbage—burn what you can, and put the remainder in the camp garbage can or bury it.

Some campers have thwarted bears by laying down a ring of moth crystals around camp, by spraying camp nightly with insecticide, or by tying a creosote-soaked rag on the door of the car trunk and locking food inside.

Booby traps are often effective: pile up a stack of tin cans, pots and pans, and rig a trip-line to them. The crash will waken you, and it may scare off the bear. If a bear comes around, make noise and flash lights. Beat pans together. He may go on to the next camping party.

UNEXPECTED COMPANY for lunch? Bears in campgrounds are after food. Don't argue with them.

FIRST AID

Although it is unlikely that he will have to face an emergency, the prudent camper is prepared to cope with sudden illness or accident. He may have to be his own doctor, and he will urgently need to know the basic principles of first aid. Ideal preparation for this is the standard Red Cross First Aid course (see your local Red Cross chapter). Carry a first aid handbook or a Boy Scout manual in your first aid kit.

In camp, a few precautions are just common sense. Set rules for children about wandering away from camp, playing around water, wearing wet clothing. If there is a possibility of poisonous snakes in the vicinity, everyone should know how to avoid them.

Serious emergencies

If you are camping in organized areas, medical help is usually not far away in case of serious illness or injury. Know how to get in touch with the rangers; they will usually take over from there.

The camper should, however, know how to handle the four emergencies that require immediate treatment to prevent death. Each of these conditions should be referred to a doctor as quickly as possible.

1. Where blood is flowing from a cut artery or vein. (Apply pressure.)

2. Where breathing has stopped. (Apply artificial respiration.)

3. Where a poisonous substance has been eaten. (Induce vomiting with 4 or 5 glasses of lukewarm soapsuds, salt water, soda water, dishwater; rinse stomach with 2 or 3 glassfuls of water. If poison was a burning or corrosive substance, give milk, or milk and raw eggs after vomiting. Treat for shock.)

4. Where serious shock is present. (Put feet 18 inches higher than head, keep injured person warm with blankets, hot water bottle.)

What not to do

Don't overdo the use of a tourniquet. First aid instructions are often written with the assumption that the victim will be attended by a doctor within a very short time, but this isn't always possible in a remote camp. If you must use a tourniquet, loosen it every 15 to 20 minutes—for it may do more harm than the wound you are treating.

Many doctors believe that a tourniquet should not be used for wounds below the elbow or knee. Most of these can be controlled if the limb is kept raised above the heart and a bandage held tightly over the open wound. If you are alone and must control severe bleeding from a wound in the lower leg, try to stop it with a pressure bandage and use a tourniquet only if the bandage fails. Lie down and keep the leg elevated. If you have to walk back to camp, apply a tourniquet if the pressure bandage does not contain the bleeding, but be sure to loosen it every 15 minutes.

Don't move injured persons unnecessarily. Wait until a trained person arrives to supervise treatment.

Don't give liquids to unconscious persons.

Don't give a cathartic or emetic to persons with severe cramps or vomiting.

Don't neglect to call a doctor immediately when a serious condition exists.

Simple injuries and ailments

Study your first aid book ahead of time and learn how to take care of simple injuries and ailments.

Campers should try to avoid getting sunburned, as severe burns are very painful. Burning occurs more easily at high altitudes, on hazy days, and in light terrain such as sandy beach, snow, or desert.

Learn how to care for sprains, and how to treat heel blisters, infections, simple burns, nose bleed, and faintness.

If there will be fishing, carry wire-cutters and antiseptic in the fishing kit so a hook caught in the skin can be cut for removal. Clean the wound thoroughly and treat with antiseptic.

For earache apply heat and have the patient chew gum to keep passages open. The cause may be an insect, so shine a flashlight into the ear; light usually brings out an offending bug.

For diarrhea give pectin medicine for immediate treatment; cut down on fruit and increase dairy products. Give plenty of water to prevent dehydration. Pollen in the local water supply may be the cause; if so, you may have to get drinking water elsewhere, as boiling will not remove the pollen.

A change in diet or altitude sometimes causes constipation, particularly in the mountains. To relieve symptoms, take a laxative or milk of magnesia tablets. Increase fruits in the diet and cut down on chocolate and dairy products. Drink plenty of water.

Heat reactions

Learn the difference between heat cramps, heat exhaustion, and sunstroke, and the treatment for each. Best preventive measures: Don't overdo in the heat. Rest in the shade frequently on the trail. Drink plenty of water to offset perspiration loss, and use salt tablets sparingly.

Heat cramps are usually the result of excessive perspiration and loss of salt. Prevention and remedy are the same: drink salt water (¼ teaspoon per quart) or take salt tablets. Too many tablets can also cause cramps.

Heat exhaustion is just too much heat, and is a form of shock. Body temperature drops and heart action weakens (but speeds up), accompanied by paleness, clammy skin, dizziness, possibly cramps. Treatment: Have patient rest in a cool place, feet raised and head lowered, and cover him with a blanket. Give him hot drinks, preferably with sugar.

Sunstroke is rare, but very serious. A doctor should be called immediately. The body's heat-regulating system breaks down and the onset of symptoms may be rapid—headache, flushed face, pounding pulse. Temperature mounts rapidly, the skin is hot and dry, perspiration ceases, and the patient loses consciousness. Treatment: Call a doctor without delay. Move the person into the shade and do everything you can to cool him off. Remove most of his clothing. Pour or spray his body with cold water, or even snow if available. Continue sponge baths until temperature returns to normal.

Plant irritants

The leaves, woody parts, even the flowers and berries, of poison oak, ivy, and sumac contain a substance, urushiol, which causes skin irritation and itching. Itchy red rashes and blisters may develop. You can get the rash by touching the plant, smoke from burning plants, or by contact with an article of clothing or animal which has touched it.

Learn to identify these plants and avoid them. Poison ivy grows east of the Rockies as either a climbing plant on trees and poles or as a low, shrubby, crawling plant. Poison oak, common in most western states, is more shrub-like and grows primarily in the foothills. Both have leaves in characteristic groups of three. Poison sumac is a shrub or small tree, taller and more willowy.

If exposed to one of these plants, wash the exposed parts as soon as possible with plenty of hot water and a strong, lathering soap. If convenient, wash thoroughly with rubbing alcohol, rinse in clear water, and dry. Then cover with a dressing soaked with a solution of baking soda or Epsom salts.

Calomine lotion may be applied to reduce itching. Avoid using oily ointments or scratching the rash; you only spread the irritation.

Mountain sickness

A rapid ascent from near-sea-level elevations into the mountains sometimes causes mountain sickness in persons who have not acclimatized themselves. This can occur in a car while climbing a high pass, or because of too much activity the first few days of camping. Symptoms are usually headache, nausea, and dizziness, but more serious onslaughts may cause illness, weakness, and diarrhea. Symptoms may occur the first night in camp or not for several days. Usually the person improves with rest and sedentary pastimes, but if illness persists, he should return to lower altitudes.

Some normal body functions, especially in women, are upset temporarily by changes in altitude, and such disturbances should not cause great concern.

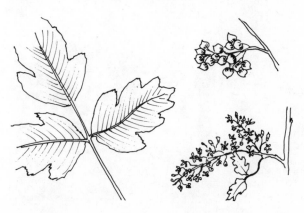

POISON OAK is a pest in all seasons. You can get a rash from its leaves, berries, flowers, even bare branches.

Recreational vehicles

Perhaps you have tired of auto camping, and although you still enjoy the out-of-doors, you would prefer to camp more comfortably. Possibly your family requires facilities and equipment which conventional camping does not afford. Maybe you prefer to camp in a variety of places, but dislike the thought of constantly making and breaking camp. Whatever your reason, let us assume you are considering some specialized vehicle to make camping easier or more convenient.

The recreational vehicle market is booming, with the industry now producing over a half million per year. In the larger campgrounds through-out the West, the majority of campers use some type of recreational vehicle; you see them everywhere. And you have a wide variety from which to choose.

Try rentals first. Purchase of one of the larger units represents a major investment. If you plan to use your vehicle only one or two weeks a year, you will pay a high price on a cost-per-day basis. In addition to original cost, you must consider depreciation, taxes, financing charges, licensing, maintenance, and other expenses. You may have a problem storing your vehicle when not in use.

Today almost any kind of recreational vehicle has a high resale value. Many dealers rent new ones the first year, then sell them. Rentals range from less than $35 a week for small camping trailers to more than $250 a week for a big motor home—although in the off season you can probably do a little better. You can even fly to Hawaii or Alaska and have your reserved camper waiting for you at the airport. No doubt this service will become common elsewhere.

Your choice of vehicle depends a great deal upon your own preferences, your pocketbook, the size of your family, and your car. A compact sedan with a relatively small motor can tow the lightweight camping trailer or perhaps the smallest size travel trailer. If your car is larger you have more latitude. Should you have a pickup truck, you can rent a camper body for it by the week.

CAMPING (TENT) TRAILERS

The early models were merely lightweight trailers with a low silhouette which unfolded into two full-size beds. A hinged framework supporting a tent rose upward and outward to provide shelter. On some of them the closed cover had two levels, forming a base for the beds and also allowing some storage space.

These small vehicles offered several conveniences lacking in car camping. Once the trailer

RENTAL CAMPER awaits arriving Hawaii vacationers. Camper comes with bedding and towels.

WEEKENDING FAMILIES park campers at the beach and unload table, chairs, and hamper for a picnic. Campers are popular in beach parks; they provide protection and self-contained facilities.

was spotted in the desired position at the camp-site, the tent could be put up in a matter of moments. Beds were ready for use simultaneously with erection of the tent, without the bother of setting up cots or inflating air mattresses. The trailer body provided a solid floor, easier to keep clean than a tent floor, and in case of stormy weather it was possible to cook in it. People who were unused to the out-of-doors felt more secure in them.

From the beginning the tent trailer enjoyed considerable popularity. In the intervening years, as sales mounted and competition for this new market increased, there have been many design innovations. They are no longer called tent trailers, but camping trailers. You can still buy a small one very similar to the early tent trailer, which without any options costs around $300. Or you can go the

deluxe route and spend in the neighborhood of $2,000 for a large camping trailer with all the options; this version has almost the same conveniences as the shortest rigid-construction travel trailers. In fact, the cost of the largest camping trailer overlaps that of the compact travel trailers.

General features

Despite more complex framing and greater weight, these newer type trailers open about as easily and quickly as the early models. The hard-top roof, which may be aluminum, steel, fiberglass, or one of the rugged, modern, shaped plastics, gives better heat insulation, is unlikely to leak, and will take the brunt of even the heaviest hail storm. Its greatest advantage, however, is that it creates

COMBINATION of station wagon and tent trailer makes camping easy. Mother cooks on a portable stove on the wagon tailgate, family eats outside on drop-down shelf, sleeps inside tent trailer.

a complete small room in which you can walk around with adequate head clearance, with the sleeping compartments in "lean-tos" at either end.

The flat roof makes it possible to turn the interior body area into a small combination eating-cooking room. Collapsible screen doors come with the unit, and some openings may have auxiliary transparent windows of plastic which can be zipped closed. Fittings are luxurious, with vinyl floors, settees in gay colors, built-in sinks and water tanks, gas stoves and ice boxes with capacity up to a 25-pound block of ice, dinettes, storage cabinets, and electric lights.

In floor space, convenience, and comfort, the more expensive camping trailers compete fairly well with a travel trailer of equal cost. A minor disadvantage is the time required to set them up on arrival and close them again on departure.

Some facilities are less convenient than in a rigid-walled trailer because they must be arranged to fit beneath the low cover in traveling. Access is difficult when the unit is closed.

The low walls of the camping trailer restrict wall storage and other niceties, and there is limited space to carry equipment not included with the unit. In cold or rainy weather the canvas walls of the folding-type trailer may get clammy, and heating will be a problem. But in good weather the walls can be opened wide, making them less confining.

Sizes and prices

The ease and comfort provided by a big camping trailer, compared to conventional auto camping, is obvious. Usually camping trailers can be taken into rough country and readily spotted on a campsite. They are easy to tow on the highway, are little affected by side winds, and do not obstruct rear vision from the towing vehicle.

In weight they go up to about 1,200 pounds—and will carry another 400 pounds of equipment. This is four-fifths of a ton; if you are carrying several people and an additional load in the towing vehicle, engine power is an important factor.

Deluxe camping trailers have probably reached their limit in size. Large ones will sleep up to eight people; they are adequate for most families. Minor refinements will be added from time to time. Any changes in these two factors will affect their market advantages versus the travel trailers. Certainly if you are considering purchase of a large camping trailer, you should compare it very carefully with travel trailers in the same price range.

Below the $1,000-$1,200 level the hard top disappears, along with most of the accessories, and you are back to the older type tent trailer. Some have clever arrangements—like a stove which can be used either outside or inside, and dinette arrangements which make into an extra bed—but in the lower priced units you are primarily buying sleeping space and shelter. In this range the more expensive tent trailers are simply larger, and may be of sturdier, more attractive construction. They claim to sleep six comfortably, which may be a mild exaggeration unless some are children.

All the smaller size camping trailers sleep four; beds are about the same size as in the larger trailers, and they carry 400 pounds of extra luggage as the large ones do. Prices range from $500 to $750, with additional cost for optional equipment.

At least one company offers an economy line of neat, serviceable tent trailers in the $350-$400 range. For about $250 this same company also offers a slide-in box for a pickup which folds out to make two double beds in a tent.

Things to look for

Good brakes and sturdy tires are important on the heavier trailers. Some state laws require brakes on all trailers with a gross weight of 1,500 pounds, while one or two states stipulate 1,000 pounds. Balance is also important—a fact to keep in mind when you load. Devices for leveling should be

---

WHAT ARE WE TALKING ABOUT?

Let's define the various recreation vehicles we are considering:

Camping (tent) trailer. Lightweight (250-1,200 lbs.) two-wheeled low trailer intended only for camping. Folds out to make a tent with beds, sometimes a partially roofed structure with canvas walls. *Advantages*: low cost, light weight, mobility. *Disadvantages*: limited facilities in smaller models.

Travel trailer. House trailer of shorter lengths, roughly 12 to 30 feet, can be towed by a conventional automobile. *Advantages*: better organization of space. *Disadvantages*: lack of mobility in larger models.

Pickup camper. Used only on pickup trucks, ½ or ¾-ton almost exclusively, usually slide-in but may be chassis-mounted. Wide variety of styles. *Advantages*: approaches travel trailer convenience with better mobility. *Disadvantages*: high center of gravity, difficulties in floor arrangement inherent in narrow slide-in base, entire vehicle must be driven even on short drives.

Camper van. Evolved from the small delivery vans with engine slung low beside driver's seat. Are really small motor homes. *Advantages*: mobility, can be used as all-purpose car. *Disadvantages*: cramped, except for small family.

Motor home. Similar to travel trailer except mounted on a truck chassis with its own motive power and controls. *Advantages*: luxury travel. *Disadvantages*: bulky to maneuver.

---

simple and easy to operate. With the trailer box closed on the road, you should be able to lock it, in case you want to stop en route.

Options

You may never need them, but a spare tire and wheel will add only a minor amount to the total cost. If you go to campgrounds where electrical hookups are provided—and most private ones catering to trailers and campers have them—it is convenient to have wiring and a socket for connecting to a conventional 110-volt line. With a few extensions you can have lights wherever you want

IN SOME CAMPGROUNDS you can rent small trailers and have them spotted at your campsite.

them, and also use small electrical appliances. Most manufacturers offer canopies; some have a sizable screened room which fastens to the main structure.

Towing

Except for the heaviest models, you can tow camping trailers with almost any passenger car. The National Safety Council recommends that for safety the trailer being towed should weigh less than half the weight of the car.

Most states have reduced speed laws for trailers; but even at legal speeds, too heavy a trailer can throw a light car out of control if it begins whipping. Vertical whipping also can occur, although it is less apparent.

TRAVEL TRAILERS

With the publicity pickup campers and camping trailers have received in the past few years, the travel trailer appears to have lost some ground, although the total sold still exceeds that of either camping trailers or pickup campers. Many people dismiss the travel trailer because they feel it would slow them down, but you may find you get more vehicle for your money with a travel trailer than with either of its two major competitors.

General features

Today's travel trailer is essentially a simple box shape. This rectangle allows good use of floor space and avoids the arrangement difficulties of a collapsible unit. Its interior is well organized, with many ingenious places for wall storage. It has a low center of gravity.

In cold weather it is easy to heat, although it can be hard to keep cool on hot days. Adequate window space is difficult to provide in rigid-walled vehicles (including campers) because the strength of the construction is in the walls themselves.

Travel trailer sizes range from compacts about 12-13 feet long to those around 30 feet in length, increasing by 1-foot increments. Larger sizes merge into the mobile home category. Both costs and weight increase with length, although the use of modern materials has helped in weight reduction. Vehicles of comparable size should weigh approximately the same. Techniques have been fairly well standardized, and although one vehicle may have innovations not found in another, good construction sets a minimum on size, cost, and weight.

While you may buy a compact for less than the cost of the largest camping trailers, you can expect to pay around $5,000 for one of the big travel trailers—without options. These can add another $1,000—up to $1,500 if you elect an air conditioner. On a package deal—buying one of these big trailers new—you should get some discount on the options.

For this money you receive a luxurious traveling apartment, with kitchen facilities comparable to those at home; a bath with shower, tub, and flush toilet; hot and cold running water; and comfortable sleeping space for four, with room for two more if needed.

You have also removed yourself from the auto camping category, and have limited yourself in most cases to the specialized privately operated campgrounds catering to big trailers. These long and heavy trailers are difficult to maneuver; their low clearance is also a handicap, particularly in traveling over secondary roads. Most public campgrounds have neither the space nor the facilities for the big units.

A few state parks and some national parks have trailer villages with hookup facilities for electricity, water, and plumbing; an extra fee is charged for their use. However, usually these facilities are only in private parks catering to the larger trailers.

Sizes and prices

The 30-foot trailer represents about the maximum size for any of the recreation vehicles, and it is recreational only in the sense that travel is recreation. The investment is considerable; purchasers of this large model are often retired people with enough leisure time to make the investment worthwhile.

Dealers say that in today's market the 16 or 17-foot travel trailer sells best—despite attempts by various manufacturers to reach a lower-priced market with smaller 12 or 13-foot compacts. Although the price differential is considerable—compact around $1,150 versus about $2,500 for the larger models—buyers prefer the larger size.

You cannot range as freely with it as you can with a camping trailer. Weight of a 16-footer without load will be about 2,500 pounds. To this must be added the weight of any water in the tanks, ice in the icebox, extra equipment, and supplies. Total weight will be in excess of 1½ tons.

In return for restricting your travels, you will get a portable structure capable of seating and sleeping four or six people. Your butane stove will be almost full sized, with three or four burners and a built-in oven; there will also be a small refrigerator. You will have many small extra touches such as magazine racks, additional lights, sizable closet, shower and toilet, as well as extra floor space and more storage space.

Plumbing and electrical wiring will be dual purpose, so your unit can use outside hookups or be self-contained. Your vehicle will have fresh water tanks, and a holding tank for sewage and waste water (optional on smaller sizes). The piping can shift these services over if outside hookups are available in a trailer camp. In the same way, electrical wiring will handle both 12 and 110 volts.

Things to look for

The trailer and mobile home industry is expanding rapidly, and many new lines are coming onto the market each year.

Fall and winter are good times to buy. Look for second-hand travel trailers which have been rented that season. They are often "like new" at a 10 per cent savings.

Within the space available, is the kitchen workspace usable, with some counter space? Double sinks are touted, but will you have two impracticably small sinks versus a usable-sized larger one? Is the kitchen work area out of the traffic area, or placed where everyone entering or leaving the vehicle will interfere with the cook? Are there cupboards or shelves for dishes?

Undersealing is important, particularly in wet climates. Also look at floor coverings, upholstery, and counter coverings. Are they heavy weight or will they wear quickly? Metal joints should be used between the sheets of interior covering. Are window openings well located, sturdy, and easily opened? Jalousies permit more air but may not seal well. Roof vents are vital in hot weather. Can additional vents be installed as an option? How good is the insulation?

TRAILER TIPS

You must learn a different set of road rules when piloting a trailer. State laws usually require you to travel at slower speeds. Your car will not have its customary pick-up, so allow more time and a longer stretch of road for passing. Greater momentum makes stopping slower. When you see a long row of cars lining up behind you, especially on a hill, pull over at the first wide spot and signal them by. Some states have a law requiring you to pull over and let traffic pass if a number of cars queue up behind you. Pullouts are marked.

Unless you are preparing to pass, you must allow at least 500 feet between you and the vehicle ahead, making it easier for an overtaking car to pass.

Check your equipment frequently, especially the hitch, lights, and tires. When driving, watch for sway or the peculiar weaving motion known as "fish-tailing". Normally the trailer will track well behind your car. Sway often means too much weight in the rear of the trailer. About 10 per cent of the weight should be on the hitch. Fish-tailing is sometimes caused by steering with too light a hand (try to keep your steering wheel steady) or by strong cross winds.

Backing with a trailer seems difficult at first, but it just takes practice. Pick an open area and practice a few times. Always back up slowly and, whenever possible, try to back around to the left so you can see what's behind the trailer.

You can expect to use from one-fourth to one-half more gasoline when pulling a trailer. Heavier cars will show a smaller proportionate increase in gasoline consumption than the light cars. Pound for pound, increased gasoline consumption for a camper or trailer will be about the same.

In many mountainous localities, there are firms that specialize in towing trailers over difficult grades. You can save wear and tear on your car by hiring a truck to pull your trailer over any passes that might put a strain on the family car. Check with service stations at the foot of the grade.

Insurance and registration. Read your policy carefully or check with your insurance company before hooking onto any trailer. The liability and property damage provisions of your car insurance will apply to a trailer, but not the collision, fire and theft, or comprehensive provisions.

State license and registration fees are based on the value of the trailer. The license fee decreases with the trailer's age, but the registration fee remains fixed.

Are corner frame members strong and carefully joined? Good trailer construction should be like that of a ship. It is subject to considerable twisting. so must be resilient to absorb stresses.

Options

Canvas awnings and auxiliary screened rooms are also available to fit on the side of a travel trailer. You should definitely carry a spare wheel and tire. A gas burning light can save electricity.

Many of the options on smaller travel trailers are included as standard equipment on the larger units. Instead of an ice box you may have a gas refrigerator. A combination gas-electric type is also available; when you have no outside electricity source you use gas, and switch over to electricity when available.

There are expensive additions such as air conditioning, built-in hi-fi, and your own electricity generator. You also have options on the kind of toilet, the size of the holding tank, and water supply.

If you plan to keep your trailer in a garage, you might consider a model with a lower roof. This means slightly less headroom inside, but you can use the trailer as an extra guest room (or study). Another model lowers over its wheelbase for garage parking.

Towing

The same general rules apply for travel trailers as for camping trailers; since they represent a heavier load, the rules are even more important. You may need heavier shock absorbers on the rear of your car, overload springs, or equalizing hitches. Discuss this in detail with the trailer dealer from whom you rent or buy. And you should also do a little outside checking on your own to make sure the trailer you are considering is not too heavy for your car to tow.

PICKUP CAMPERS

The pickup camper (usually called, simply, camper) apparently was a California invention, at first used only by sportsmen. It is still most common in the West. Early campers were homemade of plywood, primarily to provide a convenient place to sleep. As urban areas expanded, hunters

LOADED CAMPERS may be slow and hold back traffic. Pull over at the first turnout and let others pass.

and fishermen had to travel increasingly greater distances to enjoy their sports. With a camper a man could leave after work on Friday, travel directly to his chosen spot that evening without worrying about motels or setting up camp, and be out stalking or fishing at dawn Saturday.

The camper is unique because it is directly tied to one type of vehicle—the pickup truck. It originally evolved because so many sportsmen already had pickup trucks for traveling the back roads; today many people who would not otherwise own a pickup buy one solely to mount a camper on it.

Enthusiasm for the camper has not been lost on manufacturers; throughout the country many companies now produce them. Some manufacturers are trailer-makers who have discovered campers as a profitable new line. Just as there are more pickup campers in the West, there are more camper manufacturers in the West, with California the leader in production.

General features

Campers can be anything from a "shell", or "cap", or "liner", costing a few hundred dollars, to the huge cabover, chassis-mounted types costing thousands of dollars and offering much the same luxury as a motor home. The shell is simply a section that fits above the sides of the pickup to enclose the body, usually with a back panel fitted with a door. Made of aluminum or fiberglass, sometimes canvas on a frame, some insulated and some not, they are easily fitted and relatively inexpensive—without refinements they cost $300 to $400. For a little more money you can get a larger shell and a few simple refinements, such as a folding table and padded seats; but at this point your shell is beginning to turn into a camper.

A pickup fitted with a simple shell is often overlooked as a camping vehicle. If you don't want to spend too much money, it has many points in its favor as a compromise second car.

In the mountains or in rough terrain the pickup is far superior to the conventional station wagon. It has stronger springs, more clearance, and better visibility from the higher driver's seat. Its serviceability is proven by its popularity with highway departments, park and forest agencies, and construction crews.

A pickup with a shell will carry a much larger load than a station wagon. With an adequate engine you will have no trouble taking the load over terrain too difficult for a passenger car. At the campsite the body is a convenient refuge in a sudden storm, and it will even furnish emergency sleeping quarters for several children and adults.

The simple shell is actually less a camper than a light, covered truck. Some handyman owners fit them with bunks and cooking facilities, changing them into primitive campers. You will find this development most often among inveterate hunters and fishermen who pursue their hobbies in all weather.

After the shell come the various kinds of true pickup campers. These are travel trailers constructed to fit into and around the pickup body. They come in a number of lengths, but the width is the same for all. Automobile manufacturers have standardized pickup body sizes.

Some manufacturers make a slightly longer body for the longer campers, with sturdier suspension. In fact, options are available on almost all pickups which make them more suitable for carrying a camper.

The camper's advantage over the travel trailer is its mobility. The larger campers have a higher center of gravity, which means road speeds should be decreased. Two experienced drivers, one with a light travel trailer and the other with a heavy cabover pickup camper, would probably travel about the same speed on the road.

Trailer owners argue they can leave their trailer locked on the campsite, retaining their area, while they explore the surrounding country in their automobile or go to town for supplies. Pickup camper owners cannot do this without removing the camper from the pickup—a laborious and even dangerous process without good jacks. Few care to do it for such short periods. (Many owners do remove them at home so they can use the pickup without the camper, but there is a storage problem just as with a trailer.) A small travel trailer and a camper are in the same price range, but there is more usable space in the trailer.

Sizes and prices

The smallest campers are the eight-footers—the same length as the truck body. These box-like compartments are as wide as the truck at the top, but with a narrower lower portion which slides

---

HITCHES AND CHAINS

A simple bumper-mounted ball hitch will suffice for light loads, but for any appreciable trailer load, your car should have a frame mounted hitch.

An equalizer hitch is highly advisable when you are towing several thousand pounds. This spreads the load between the rear wheels of the towing vehicle as well as on the trailer wheels.

Safety chains will be legally required almost anywhere you go with a trailer of any size. You should use only coil-steel welded chain with manufacturer-supplied repair links or supplementary welds. At least 3/16-inch chain should be used for Class I trailers, ¼-inch for Class II, and 5/16-inch for Class III. (The chain must be strong enough to take the entire tow load if the hitch breaks or becomes disconnected.)

In connecting chains, equalize the slack on either side, leaving just enough for proper turning. Cross them under the tongue so that if a coupling failure occurs, the tongue will not drop to the road.

VEHICLE CAMPERS have just about taken over this Southern California beach campground. The exposed site on the ocean makes wind and sun protection desirable.

into the body. They fit into the lighter ½-ton pickups and cost from $800 to $1,000, depending on interior furnishings. They are cramped, but will have at least a stove and cooler, and sleep two to four people. These are practical for a group of men on a hunting or fishing trip, using auxiliary tents and sleeping bags, but for the camping family this compromise is not much better than a shell or a camping trailer. You can buy the whole unit, new truck and all, for about $3,000, but you should look at it very critically; you probably will wish you had bought something bigger.

After the eight-footers come the cabovers. As the name indicates, the forward part of the box extends over the top of the truck cab for more space, while the bottom still is a slide-in. This removes the master bedroom from the living area and allows more latitude in furniture arrangement. This is a big improvement, even when the basic box is still eight feet. There is more room for cooking and storage (on the road light things can be carried up forward in the cabover) and there is space for such features as a small wardrobe, dinette, settees, and kitchen cabinets.

BEACH PARK has individual camping sites with permanent table, food locker, firepit, and water supply.

Cabovers, unless they are very light, should be on ¾-ton pickups. Since the stronger chassis permits more weight, the basic box can be extended rearward up to an additional three feet, adding considerable extra-space—perhaps for a shower and toilet, refrigerator, or larger dinette. Prices may climb to $3,000 for this cabover; cost of the entire unit, including the larger truck, moves toward the $5,500-$6,000 level—and more for deluxe models. The biggest cabover campers have a sleeping capacity of six; two adults and four children would sleep very comfortably. Extra beds can be made up over the dinette or from the settees.

The largest cabovers (usually 1-ton) are chassis-mounted—that is, bolted down to the truck body as a permanent installation. Without the slide-in feature, the lower part of the camper can be as wide as the upper, because the basic pickup body is discarded. These boxes can be 15 feet or more in length; at this point the camper merges into the motor home. Many of them have access from the rear compartment to the driver's compartment just as in a motor home, and prices for the complete assembly begin to approach the cost of the smaller motor homes.

Any discussion of costs for deluxe campers is confusing, because of the various options and also the way models are measured. A camper is measured by its length from back of cab to its rear end, while a motor home is measured by its overall length. A chassis-mounted camper is probably cheaper than a comparable motor home, because the camper is built on the assembly line for mounting on stock truck chassis.

You sometimes see the camper with a telescoping box; the roof lowers several feet to fit down over the bottom portion. On the road its lower center of gravity makes for better handling, and cross winds have less effect. It will also fit easily into a garage. However, interior arrangements must be fitted to the telescoped position.

Things to look for

The first thing to consider is size. There is no point in getting a larger camper than you need, but be sure it will be adequate for your family. Bigger cabovers sleep up to six, but privacy is very limited and getting settled is awkward. You may want to carry a good tent or tow a small travel trailer as many camper owners do.

Some experienced campers find this combination more versatile without adding a great deal to

CAMPER TIPS

Your rear view mirror is useless, so adjust your side mirrors carefully; they must extend out far enough to see back on both sides of your trailer or camper.

Remember your camper is a much heavier vehicle than you are accustomed to. Allow more distance for stops.

Watch tire pressure closely. Mild over-inflation is better than under-inflation, if you are uncertain of the correct pressure. Keep opposite tires equal.

Because a rear load will tilt your headlights upward, you should adjust them for a fully loaded condition. Carry some spare bulbs for your lights. Make sure you have an adequate jack. On both trailers and campers a lost key can be serious, requiring breaking into the vehicle. Keep spares bolted on or in a magnetic case hidden somewhere on the vehicle.

Check holddowns on the body frequently. Bolts or turnbuckles may loosen. Some owners put cotter key holes in the bolts, or double nut them with lock washers.

Check the water tank on a new unit; it will probably need flushing. Don't use a new hose to fill water tanks, as it will give the water a bad taste. When you fill your tank on the road, taste the water first. Clean a bad smelling tank by dumping a half box of baking soda into it and flushing it thoroughly.

Make sure all openings in the box are closed before getting underway. The interior may get a little stuffy, but it's better than finding everything coated with dust.

Always check the LP-gas system, even on rental units. If your supply runs out, shut off everything; otherwise when you refill you may lose your entire new supply unknowingly. Leaking gas also is dangerous.

Trailer loads should be balanced, as much as possible close to the axle, with 10 per cent more weight forward than to the rear so a positive pressure is maintained on the hitch.

On a camper all the extra load should be placed as low as possible, and well forward. Do not use the cabover space for anything except light items, such as sleeping bags.

In any self-contained recreation vehicle, you must consider water tanks, holding tanks, and LP-gas tanks. On an extended trip a holding tank, as it fills, changes the load characteristics considerably. A full 40-gallon tank weighs 300 pounds more than an empty one. Tanks are best located well forward and centered on a camper; water tanks are best if centered on a trailer.

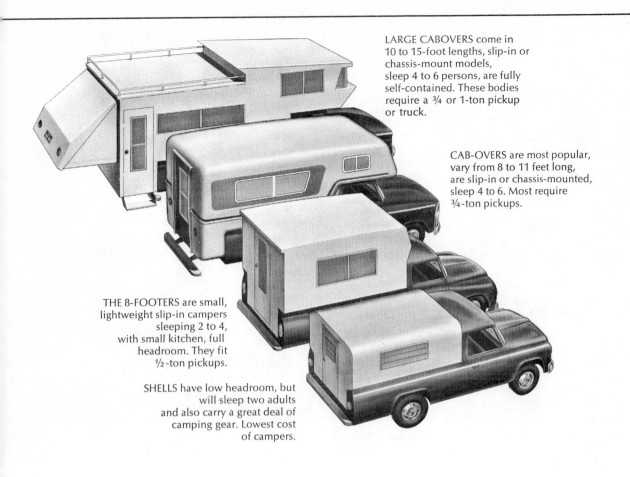

LARGE CABOVERS come in
10 to 15-foot lengths, slip-in or
chassis-mount models,
sleep 4 to 6 persons, are fully
self-contained. These bodies
require a ¾ or 1-ton pickup
or truck.

CAB-OVERS are most popular,
vary from 8 to 11 feet long,
are slip-in or chassis-mounted,
sleep 4 to 6. Most require
¾-ton pickups.

THE 8-FOOTERS are small,
lightweight slip-in campers
sleeping 2 to 4,
with small kitchen, full
headroom. They fit
½-ton pickups.

SHELLS have low headroom, but
will sleep two adults
and also carry a great deal of
camping gear. Lowest cost
of campers.

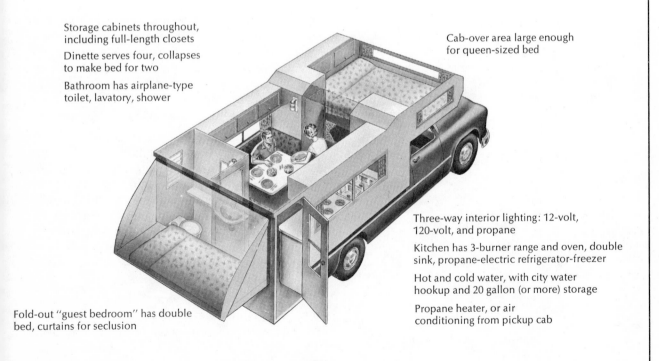

Storage cabinets throughout,
including full-length closets

Dinette serves four, collapses
to make bed for two

Bathroom has airplane-type
toilet, lavatory, shower

Cab-over area large enough
for queen-sized bed

Three-way interior lighting: 12-volt,
120-volt, and propane

Kitchen has 3-burner range and oven, double
sink, propane-electric refrigerator-freezer

Hot and cold water, with city water
hookup and 20 gallon (or more) storage

Propane heater, or air
conditioning from pickup cab

Fold-out "guest bedroom" has double
bed, curtains for seclusion

SEMI-COLLAPSIBLE CAMPER is being readied for use at the campsite. On the road, upper section is lowered (see below) for easier road handling, less sway, and better speed.

AT HOME, semi-collapsible camper is in lowered position to fit easily into the owner's garage.

the cost. They have a simple 8-foot box on the pickup, with a powerful engine, strong suspension, and a good hitch. When the entire family goes on a trip, they tow a light travel or camping trailer, or carry equipment for auto camping. The pickup can be used for side trips carrying only a light load, for two men on a weekend fishing trip, or for towing a boat.

If you plan to use your camper as a self-contained unit, you must look critically at its size in relation to your needs. Before purchase you should make several weekend trips in a rented vehicle so you will have some idea of your requirements. It is safer to err on the larger side than the smaller; the difference will probably be only a few hundred dollars, and is much cheaper than "trading up" after a year or so.

The interior arrangement is important, since you will sacrifice some space in favor of more mobility. Many of the larger campers now have side entrances, for instance, but these are not necessarily better. Look at both rear and side entrance models, and try to visualize them in camp with your own family using them.

Because of restricted space, the kitchen arrangement on a camper is particularly important. On the cabover models, is the forward bed easy to enter? When the beds are in use, will one person getting up disturb everyone?

Options

If you select a large camper, you can choose almost any option offered for a travel trailer.

If you need maximum sleeping space, look for models with a fold-out bed in the back. Another model has a hinged rear patio which drops down level with the rear door. You can purchase screening and canvas to make this area into an outdoor screened patio room or a private bedroom.

Selecting the pickup

Your dealer can be your best guide in matching a new pickup to the camper you want. All manufacturers have a wide variety of sizes available for anything from the lightest camper body to the big chassis mounts.

Since the rear components of a pickup carry a big proportion of the camper body load, the importance of matching these to the load cannot be overstressed. The engine must be powerful enough to handle the load, and the tires and suspension components are vital for ease of handling and safety. The pickup camper has the highest center of gravity of any of the recreation vehicles, so any tendency to sway and pitch is magnified.

Engines are available for pickups from 125 to 300 horsepower. You will need at least 200 horsepower for the largest campers. Engine power on a pickup is planned for more pull and lower maximum speed, and engine design also will probably have the same approach. Horsepower ratings are calculated differently for passenger cars and trucks.

On a pickup carrying a camper, you must think not only of horsepower and suspension, but also of stronger tires—10 ply on the rear for a chassis mount, and six or eight for the smaller campers. Extra engine cooling capacity is desirable, also a rugged transmission with two ratios below high gear, possibly an auxiliary battery; power steering and power brakes are recommended.

Too heavy a unit for the job is false economy,

reflected not only in initial cost but also in operating cost. But any savings on too light a combination can be more than lost both in maintenance and in convenience.

CAMPER VANS

The camper van is an outgrowth of the stub-nosed delivery van. These have been fitted out as camping vehicles in Europe for many years, and they have recently begun to gain acceptance in the United States.

They are sturdy vehicles with almost as much space inside as a small travel trailer, although higher off the ground. The engine is slung low in the front end beside the driver so the wheel base

CARRYING A BOAT

A small boat can increase your fun if you are camping near a lake or river. Modern variations of the World War II inflatable life rafts have gained great popularity for the collapsible boat.

Canoes, kayaks, and small plastic or aluminum boats are easily carried on the flat roof of a camper, trailer, or camper car. You can buy boat racks for a moderate price, or if you are handy with tools, you can make one yourself.

Supports should not be too widely spaced and should be covered with a material to prevent abrasion (such as old carpeting). Lashings should be made of light steel cable with turnbuckles for tight fastening.

BOAT is carried on roof of station wagon. You can get special carriers for boats.

can be kept short without sacrificing interior space. We talked to one man who bought a plain, panel-sided secondhand delivery van and uses it as a commute car. When the family goes camping, which they do often, the mother drives their passenger car and he the van. Children take turns riding with father and mother. The capacious interior of the van takes all their camping equipment with ease.

The first offshoot of these short wheelbase delivery vans was a many-windowed station wagon type vehicle which could seat 12. In recent years small companies all over the country have specialized in converting this "station wagon" model into recreational vehicles, and now some of the big auto manufacturers offer them through their salesrooms.

General features

The van camper can be made about as luxurious as the pickup camper, although on the smaller ones facilities will be somewhat miniaturized. These are not quite as convenient as a compact travel trailer, but they are more nimble on the road and less trouble than any of the other recreation vehicles. Virtually all state laws classify them as passenger cars or station wagons.

They can be used as passenger cars, even if fitted out for camping. The settees will accommodate several people, and there are two seats in the driver's compartment. At the campsite they are best for young couples with one or two small children, as sleeping for more than two adults is somewhat cramped. Some young couples have only one car—a van fitted out for camping which also serves as an all purpose vehicle.

As might be expected, competition has produced a great variety of designs. The major improvement, also borrowed from the European van campers, is the extendable roof. The van body itself has a roof slightly low for an adult to walk around under freely, so most models now have a lightweight raised roof, usually plastic or fiberglass. Some are pop-up with canvas sides.

Sizes and prices

With the longer wheelbase model, designers have another two feet to work with; these can make the living area more spacious. Wheelbase sizes range from about 90 to 120 inches. Costs can vary from $3,000 to more than $6,000, depending on equipment. Interior furnishings will compare with a camper or small travel trailer.

Some vans have rear pop-out extra sleeping

rooms, or special units which fit on the roof to provide an additional bed.

The camper van is really a small motor home. In its simpler form it offers a compromise between the other three types of recreation vehicles—the camping trailer, the travel trailer, and the pickup camper—and will certainly gain many enthusiasts. The larger, more luxurious models should be considered in much the same light as the larger travel trailers—although you have much more latitude in places you can go with them, their cost requires a great deal of use to merit the investment.

MOTOR HOMES

The motor home is a travel trailer built on a truck chassis. They can be very luxurious—and expensive. Body sizes range from about 18 to 28 feet; a few custom-built units are even longer. The shorter models, big box-like vehicles which clearly show their evolution from the travel trailer, are available for under $10,000; the more attractive and luxurious models, loaded with options, can cost several times that amount. The motor home is more mobile than a large travel trailer and is designed to cruise at highway speeds, so you may occasionally see one in a campground having easy access. But their cost can only be justified on trips lasting weeks or months, several times a year.

TRUCK CHASSIS STATION WAGONS

Several big auto manufacturers make rugged large-size station wagons which are mounted on a truck chassis. These are popular in rural areas and on construction jobs. Some of them can be fitted with four-wheel drive, or at least positive traction. You can also get most of the luxury options available for conventional cars.

These sturdy models ride and steer surprisingly well. Cost is about the same as for a conventional middle-priced station wagon. They will carry six passengers and a big load of equipment almost anywhere a pickup truck can because of their high clearance. Dedicated auto campers should look closely at these.

FOUR-WHEEL-DRIVE VEHICLES

American four-wheel drive vehicles dramatized their versatility under wartime conditions, and in recent years British and Japanese manufacturers have joined the competition for a share of this market.

Outdoorsmen like these vehicles, as they can be driven into rough country and used for camping either alone or with a trailer. They can be driven over rough roads and up slopes impossible for conventional cars, and they provide greater traction, especially in snow, ice, or mud.

Unfortunately, in some areas they have been used carelessly, making new roads and trails which scar the countryside and cause accelerated erosion.

Vehicles are restricted to established roads in national parks and monuments and in state parks. Use is also limited—or barred—in some national forests; check Forest Service officials for local restrictions.

LIGHT CAMPING VAN, left, and four-wheel drive vehicle, right, are used by group in unimproved area.

Index